THE FAMILY JEWELS

and other hunting and fishing tales

BUCK NEELY

ISBN: 1499240090
ISBN 13: 9781499240092

Disclaimer

Any day spent hunting or fishing is a good one and, I'm sure, can be made into a story of some kind. But not for me. I'm looking for the stories that other people won't write about. In the real world everyone is not perfect and everything does not always go as planned.

In the stories that follow, or in some of them anyway, the characters involved seem to be operating on the shadowy side of the law. This is obviously just made-up garbage. If it were true I wouldn't be able to put it in print… right?

—Right.

Therefore if anyone doesn't like the names used in this book— they were all made up. And if anything in these pages could be used in a prosecutorial manner— it's a lie, or I just misremembered.

I hope you enjoy the book!

Acknowledgments

All research and all writing for this book was done by me and me alone. Memory being such a fallible source of data there will invariably be errors, or perceived errors, about exact facts included herein. I think it best that we don't let your opinion get in the way of a good story.

My thanks go to the people who are in these stories. They put in the time and effort required to manufacture some extraordinary memories. And most of the time they had to put up with me while doing it.

Some of them are no longer with us: Wilbur Hanks, Dr. Charles L. Neely Jr., W. Dunavant Mask, Bobby Cox, George Ray Walker— my hat comes off for these fine gentlemen.

I am going to have Ted O'Brien (Zoda in the story) do my proofreading. If there are ANY errors— it is all his fault.

Thanks to all who donated photos for this book. Without you we wouldn't have many— a house fire took all of mine.

And thanks to you, gentle reader, for buying this book. Without you there would be no point.

Foreword...

Buck Neely is to hunting and fishing as Peyton Manning is to football. The sport runs so deeply through his veins that, like a champion chess player, he is planning for the next season long before he has finished the season he is presently participating in!

He was actually born 100 or more years too late as he is happiest in the woods or on the water and could absolutely do without the technological advantages now available to those who enter into the wild. Heck, he could do without a trolling motor on his boat, being just as happy to scull it himself, or without modern firearms as he is just as proficient with a bow.

His passion for the outdoors, and willingness to put to paper some of his most memorable experiences, comes naturally as he is the descendent of the greatest of all outdoor authors, Nash Buckingham.

His freshman effort, Take Me Back, is a wonderful read and, in many ways, details the road which has led him to write The Family Jewels.

The Family Jewels is not simply a collection of stories, but an homage to those he is so grateful for having in his life, ergo, "The Family Jewels", and within each chapter is a hidden lesson, a metaphor, if you will, to cherish every moment of your life.

Buck is not just my friend, but a part of me. I hope, really believe, that through his words he will become a part of you.

Ted O'Brien, Memphis, Tennessee, 2014

Table of Contents

The Electric fishermen

The problem with being a hunter, as opposed to being a golfer or tennis player or some other form of time-consuming-money-sucking-fanatical pastime, is summer. One can hunt frogs, I guess, but I'm not going to count that. A case could be made for stalking tarpon or some other large fish in shallow water but to do that very often one must live nearby such a place to do it in, and those places don't offer much in the fall and winter when the real hunting seasons are open.

One can, in most areas, go fishing –for the normal sized, regular, close to home kinds of fish –and we all do it as a means to pass the time until hunting season opens again: but it is not the same.

Sometimes, but just on the rarest of occasions, a fishing trip can be so novel in execution, and so full of action and suspense, that one can even forget what time of the year it is...

The two boys, boys at heart that is –actually young men by then, married, mortgaged, and city-bound –were good friends and had been for most all of their remembrance. It was the custom of the two to try to plan some sort of outdoors activity, usually either hunting or fishing related, for at least a few hours out of each week. Rarely were trophy fish acquired, or even sought after – nor necessarily large catches, except on occasion and by accident. Most outings were spent catching small brim on popping bugs and throwing them back, or maybe bass fishing all afternoon for only a moderate sized fish or two. Except this time— this was quite a bit different.

Henceforth and in the interest of the interested parties concerned, said young men shall be and forever shall be known by the misnomers – Smith, and Jones.

Smith worked at a local financial institution both well known and eminently respected in the mid-south. Jones was in the construction business. Although it would seem an unlikely place to get it, Smith actually instituted the particular trip in question via information gleaned from a co-worker at said respectable financial institution. The information garnered, very private and very secret information it was too, involved how to "telephone" catfish.

For those not familiar with the term it is derived from ancient times when telephones had cranking handles on the sides. Turning the handle produced a current of electricity, which had something to do with making a phone call. As with most technological advances, enterprising persons soon discovered that this current could be perverted to other uses –namely, to stun fish. Apparently a very successful method as the term has stuck to this day and it was decreed an illegal method of fishing before I was even born. So illegal, in fact, that in a lifetime around river-rats, commercial fishermen, and people who would do it if they knew how, I've never met anyone with firsthand knowledge of the process… until now.

It turns out, all they needed was an electric fence charger –something Jones already had.

Smith's voice was excited, "All you have to do is drop a wire from the negative pole over the side of the boat, and another from the positive pole off the other side. Then put a rubber band around the contact points –that makes it pulse really fast!"

Jones, having vast experience with electric fences and getting shocked, was skeptical, "How do we keep from getting shocked in a metal boat in the water?"

"Umm…yeah…right, I'll have to check on that… but we're on for Saturday –you bring the charger!"

Undaunted by doubts or any particular claim to wisdom or judgment, the two "sportsmen" met as scheduled at a lonely, out-of-the-way launching spot, along a lonely, out-of-the-way stretch of the Mississippi River.

Smith held up two coils of rubber-coated wire, "That's how we keep from shocking ourselves!"

Jones held up a long handled dip net with a large opening, "This oughta help."

The apparatus was soon deployed. It involved a twelve-volt battery, the fence charger with rubber band, and two wires. That's all –but no fish were seen right away.

As they drifted along down river the current soon carried them over a deep hole and Smith let the ground wire out so that it could touch bottom. An eruption of water sprayed over the boat as a giant catfish surfaced and tail-walked across the water in front of the boat. When he came to a stop, stunned, the great fish lay unmoving on the surface only twenty feet away— but for only about ten seconds before departing back to the depths below. The scene was repeated over and over. Occasionally Jones could get one in the net before it revived, but not often. All in all, the guys ended up with seven or eight catfish in the eight to fifteen pound class range, but they had seen more than a hundred fish. It was time to refine the technique.

Some of the fish seen had been large, this information, along with a full cooler to show for the morning's work, helped Smith enlist his dad's participation the next day.

It was deemed that two boats were essential to maximize success. The shock boat had to have a guy working the apparatus and another to drive and net. The catch boat had to have a very daring driver and an even more agile netter; therefore another unnamed person was conscripted and took the oath of secrecy.

The operation went off without a hitch. Catfish seemed to be concentrated in certain areas, and when the shock boat drifted by them –all hell broke loose. There would be multiple big fish on the surface at one time, and only a few seconds to get the net under them before they revived. It was frantic action –and some wild boat driving. Each boat carried a one hundred quart cooler and in just a short while they were filled to the top with big hump-backed channel cats, the only species that came up.

After about an hour of this they found themselves looking over their shoulders often, watching the banks, and especially the higher vantage points on those banks. They each had the feeling of being watched. Barges passed by, an occasional small boat, all very far away and uninterested. It began to dawn on them that it would be incredibly obvious to anyone watching, anyone who was curious that is, what they were up to. If a game warden checked them they were toast –no fishing poles, batteries, wires... heck, the fish even looked a little sun-burned!

Naturally, a discussion soon began as to the possible sentencing for one getting caught "telephoning". This was probably an infraction so rare, so terrible, that the media would probably get involved . . . hmmmm.

It was decided that day, many years ago, to give up "telephoning." It was kind of like cliff diving, or bungee jumping, most people don't go back for seconds.

The next weekend found Smith, and Jones, happily catching small bream and throwing them back, and waiting on the hunting seasons again.

Down River

In order for an outdoors person to reap the rewards of his or her chosen pastime it is almost universally understood that one must master, on occasion, the vagaries of nature. Wind, waves, temperature extremes—both hot and cold—rain, and topographic factors all contribute, in one way or another, to the total outdoor experience. For example: it is understood that one should be prepared for cold weather if the trip entails waterfowl hunting in most of North America. Fishing on the ocean is without question controlled by the wind and the tide. If one pursues alligators in Florida it is probably going to be warm and buggy. But there is one, and only one, all-pervading and absolute obstacle that is encountered in all parts of the planet and all sporting endeavors—MUD.

Mud can stop, delay, or make difficult any and all forays into the great outdoors. I myself am a seasoned professional at getting a wheeled vehicle hopelessly mired to the frame.

It has happened countless times and, if I am still living next year, it will happen some more. Most of the people that I hunt and fish with are nearly as good as I am. We live and work and play in areas that have ample rainfall and diverse soil types that contribute to our general sophistication on this matter. By the time I graduated from high school there were no surprises left for me as far as mud was concerned, or so I thought—until I went "down river."

The river in question is the Mississippi. It carves its way north to south through our continent while draining thirty-one states and a portion of Canada. Along the way it picks up a diverse load of sediment. Logic tells me that this is the same dirt that we all see on a daily basis. It should therefore be familiar. I don't know how, but when this sediment gets to South Louisiana it undergoes a transformation– a chemical reaction possibly. It becomes something else entirely; something sinister, dangerous even. That's what this story is about.

Venice, Louisiana is the last town at the end of the last road that follows the river on its way to the Gulf of Mexico. Built on the alluvial floodplain created over eons of time, it is the jumping-off spot for many different industries. Sport fishermen find some of the closest access in the nation to hundred fathom water here. Commercial fishermen harvest shrimp, crawfish, oysters, tuna, snapper, pogies, and anything else that will sell. The density of oilrigs, both shallow and deep, is higher than anywhere else and the support industries that service the rigs flourish. Barely above sea level and only partially protected by man-made levees, it is a small but active place.

Though the town is located at the end of the road, the river and the alluvial floodplain with it, continues on for another twenty or so miles to the lighthouse at Southwest Pass. Along the way there are countless passes and bayous that branch out into both fresh and brackish marshes interspersed with open water bays and small, dry-land hummocks where the alligators crawl out to get a tan. If one wishes to explore this country, Venice is the last place to launch a boat, get fuel, or anything else for that matter.

My post-collegiate roommate and fellow wing-shooting aficionado was named Dun Mask. Big-boned, dark-haired, and with an appetite for adventure, Dun was six foot nine and a lean two hundred and fifty pounds of muscle with size fifteen feet that helped propel him through difficult terrain. It was our desire to lengthen the legal duck-shooting season by taking advantage of the early opening date in Louisiana. Veterans of many an Arkansas, Tennessee, and Mississippi expedition, we had all the necessary equipment and, due to our relatively young ages, plenty of energy. Therefore, in the typical youthful fashion, without any advice or gleaning of information from anyone, we packed up my truck with the usual gear, hooked up to the biggest boat we could find, and headed south out of Tennessee.

Going anywhere with Dun involved sampling the local cuisine—and especially if one was in Cajun country. Two stops for local po-boys, the first with fresh-fried local oysters and the second soft-shelled crab with an unbelievable sauce, and another for a cooler of hot boiled crawfish, got us to Venice a little behind schedule—a quick dash into the local hardware store for licenses and we would launch and be on our way.

The girl at the counter looked at us as if we were an alien species. She said that she sold fishing licenses, but nobody had ever asked for a nonresident duck-hunting license: "Doan yal ha-no duk whey yu fom?"

We assured her that we did, and when the season opened we would hunt there, but right now Louisiana was the only game going. Shaking her head in disbelief, she began making calls on our behalf. The Cajun lingo was totally undecipherable to us when she spoke to someone on the phone, but somehow we soon learned that the court house, twenty miles back to the north had licenses, and that one had to "Tage de ferree" to get there.

It was getting late in the day for courthouses, forty-mile drives, and waiting for ferries— not to mention duck-scouting— and so it was decided to launch me, in the boat, to scout out tomorrow's shoot, while Dun took care of the legal issues. Launching was accomplished at the old Venice Marina and we each set out upon our appointed tasks.

I was in a twenty-three foot Mako, center console, with a two hundred horsepower Evinrude on the back. Both boat and motor were ancient, but serviceable, and needed in order to cover a lot of territory along the big river and bayous in that area. Taking a right out of the marina eventually put me on a path down Tiger Pass. This area was all fresh water, lily pads, hydrilla, ducks and posted signs. There was not enough time to decipher what might be truly posted or otherwise and so I spun her around and headed back to the main river. Going south about ten miles there was not a lot of promising terrain until I came to Head of Passes. Here there was Pass a Loutre, South Pass, and Southwest Pass to choose from. It looked more "ducky" on the east side and so I turned the bow down Pass a Loutre and began exploring the many winding bayous and canals that intersected the pass.

It was tricky going for the big boat with lots of mud-bars and shallow water. Taking it slow—running aground by myself out here might turn into a very real survival issue—I soon came upon a large bay literally teeming with ducks of all species. Through the binoculars could be seen redheads, pintails, bluewings, canvasbacks, mallards, mottled ducks— anything and everything— and they were trading back and forth between huge rafts containing many thousands more. About a half mile from my canal, and all by itself, there stood a small patch of roseau cane that many of the birds flew right over. This would be the perfect spot—the water was obviously very shallow and all that we would have to do was walk out there, dragging a few bags of decoys, and have a great shoot. With that good feeling that comes when a great plan comes together I turned the bow of the Mako up current and sped off into the glow from the setting sun.

Dun was at the ramp waiting when I pulled up. Licenses secured, he had also purchased two pirogues with paddles from a yard sale along the way. These boats were of the extra lightweight, pointed, one-person variety and looked like they would be perfect for the job at hand. Dun's eyes gave off a predatory gleam in the looming darkness when I told him about all the ducks I had seen and the perfect spot to shoot them from. We immediately started to load our gear, now augmented by pirogues, into the big boat in preparation for an early start in the pe-dawn of the morrow.

Lodging was obtained on a nearby houseboat but there was no restaurant at the marina in those days, which necessitated a trip into town in search of more local cuisine. We settled on the Last Stop Café, the only place in town, and trusted the waitress's advice—seafood stuffed baked potato. When they came, right as we were finishing four dozen fresh-shucked oysters with crisp Saltine crackers and incredibly cold frost-covered beer, we gasped—they were huge! Filling the large, oval shaped plates were two football-sized potatoes, baked to perfection and split at the top, with insides scooped out and mixed with mountains of fresh-pulled blue crab and steaming boiled shrimp. On top of this was a layer of chopped shallots and a homemade garlic-sour cream. It was a tough job but we cleaned the plates and staggered back to the houseboat for some very sound slumber.

The next morning found us in the dark, carefully feeling our way down river through some light fog. "Carefully" is a key word here as the mouth of the Mississippi can be a busy place night or day. Cargo ships from all over the world and pilot boats operate 24/7 and take no more notice of a twenty-three foot boat than the ever-present mosquitoes. Consequently we hugged the west bank all the way down, watching out for the steep, six-foot waves generated by the pilot boats as they sped to and fro servicing the oil rigs. Finally reaching the Head of Passes and across from our destination, we picked a gap and shot across.

It was just at the grey, pre-dawn time when we entered the canal that I had marked with a pair of crossed sticks on the previous day. It felt like taking a step back in time: Voices of the myriad denizens croaked and chirped their chorus in all directions—wings thundered and water flew while the omnipresent insect chorus kept time. Clearly this area was reminiscent of the primordial soup of old.

We took this waterway a couple of miles, motor trimmed up and creeping along, until we came to the spot on the bank where I had driven in a stake the afternoon before. Here we unloaded our gear on the spoil bank that separated us from the bay we were going to hunt, donned our waders— even though it was not cold— loaded guns, ammo, and decoys into the pirogues and prepared to drag them the short, half-mile walk to our shooting spot. Young, tough, and thoroughly "carbed", we had no inkling of what was about to occur.

Eager to get with it, Dun left before me dragging his heavily laden pirogue up and over the spoil bank. I was still organizing my gear back at the boat when I heard some unprintable words followed by some muffled splashing/slurping/sucking type noises. I had to climb up and over the bank a couple of steps in order to see what was happening. There was big Dun, covered in mud, lying on the bank—gasping. He had only been out of sight a couple of minutes.

Envisioning alligator battles or cottonmouth water moccasins, I was looking intently at the area around my own feet when I asked him, "You Ok?"

"No," he stated emphatically, "There is NO BOTTOM... NONE! I didn't get ten feet!"

I was looking at his ten foot pathway through the mud that was just now beginning to close up and level out, a smooth blackish-grey surface, benign and innocent looking. "How did you get out?"

"Swam out, sort of... the water is about an inch deep and the pirogues can't even float."

Hmmmm... if Dun, at six foot nine and with leg muscles to match was having trouble then this was an entirely new and undocumented species of mud.

By then it had started to get light and we could see that ducks were trading heavily over our spot. They beckoned to us, taunting...we had to figure out a way. Lady, my trusted Labrador, who came on any and all excursions and who was standing as if on point—staring out across the bay… gave a low and soulful wine.

That did it. We were young, we were strong, and we were going to get out there! And it was also going to have to be in the pirogues which were only about seven feet long and a little over a foot wide. They were definitely not built to haul a lot of gear and so some prioritizing was in order.

Dun carried his gun, a box of shells, and twelve decoys stacked behind, in front, and under his knees. I started with the same load and Lady following but almost immediately had to jettison some decoys and make room for her; an experienced, five year old Labrador, in good shape, and she was just not going to make it. It should have been a warning.

The original "mogational" technique was to sit flat in the bottom of the boat, lean forward, plant the paddle in the mud and pull the boat forward about a foot, and then switch sides and do it again. It used every muscle in your body, all at once, and I believe if I could patent the maneuver it would sell on a TV exercise program. There was no momentum, no glide so to speak, because the boats were not floating. Furthermore, the rounded bottoms of the pirogues' interiors, as well as the paddles, decoys, dog, and ourselves were soon covered in a layer of slippery, evil smelling goo that, I believe, would be difficult to sell on television.

We made it about a hundred yards before Dun came up with "mogational technique number two," which turned out to be the method of choice. With his right knee planted in the center of the craft, palms braced on the gunwales on each side, other leg held outside the boat, he found that he could swing the free leg forward and get a much stronger and longer push. Furthermore, if one used a very high activity level the process could be performed rapidly, even occasionally to the point of generating momentum!

We were both sweating buckets under our mud coatings when we made it to the roseaus. For the first few minutes our main activity was breathing, but soon the sounds of duck wings revived us to our duty. Feeling around with a paddle, it appeared that the root system of the cane might hold us up. This would be a great help for shooting accuracy—standing up rather than sitting in a tiny, greased, round-bottomed pirogue— but it was no go. The only thing that stopped me was my armpit, hooked over the side of the boat.

Not moving a muscle from his seat during this experiment on my part, and looking somewhat pleased, Dun just said, "Told ya."

Getting back in the craft, I managed to fill it with a lot more mud, completely covering my beloved shotgun, a fact that caused me some anxiety. I was shooting a Remington 870, and Dun a Browning BPS, both reliable weapons that were known to function well in most adverse conditions, but this, it seemed, was more than the manufacturers could have foreseen.

We threw out a handful of decoys on either side of the canes, which grew in a clump of probably twenty feet in diameter. It then took some time to wipe enough mud off of the weapons and clear the barrels of obstruction with pieces of the surrounding cane before finally we could load up.

Ducks were flying over us constantly and the first shot was taken by Dun. Redheads, driven by a twenty-knot wind off the Gulf and flying in tight formation, came screaming by and he took out the leader with his second shot. The bird folded cleanly but because of its speed ended up about a hundred yards away. True to her breeding, Lady was after it immediately but was unable to run or hop. She got scared and started to panic. I was just in the act of getting situated for a boat rescue when she figured it out—with her belly flat in the mud she could slowly "swim" along in a manner that looked somewhere between an alligator and a snake. As long as she didn't try to hop, or push down, she could slither in slow motion. The retrieve took about ten minutes and completely exhausted her.

It was clear that bird retrieval was going to be a major issue and so we decided to shoot at only shots that would hopefully fall very near. We had plenty of opportunities and to help savor the moment, we took turns shooting and only shot one bird of each species per limit. It was a grand and memorable experience unlike any that either of us had witnessed before and we wanted to make it last for a while. Too long in fact… the tide had fallen and pulled what little water we had with it. This was brought to our attention on the last duck. It was my shot, a drake pintail, and when it hit the surface there was no splash… just a splunk. The bird was stuck head down in the mud with his tail sticking straight up, wiggling.

It was with a certain rising degree of trepidation that I informed Dun of the obvious: "Dun, the… our… let's try to get out of here if we still can."

Neither of us wished to spend the next twelve hours lying in the mud waiting on the tide to come back and so our departure was rapid.

Dun said that he would swing wide and pick up a drake canvasback that had fallen too far out to risk the dog and I was to pick up the decoys. If all went well we would meet at the canal.

I didn't know it earlier, but that inch or two of water had acted hugely in our favor. Without it the difficulty had at least doubled—the "side-kick" method was not working nearly as well and I was starting to get cramps. It was mandatory to come up with a new method that I will now call the "frog" method of pirogue propulsion.

First, one must develop a strong, time-is-nothing-to-me, mental attitude. Next, you must lie down flat on your stomach with both legs dangling off one end of the pirogue– some padding is advisable here. The legs should be splayed out frog-like to the sides—whence comes the name. In order to move, you draw your legs forward, sliding across the surface of the mud, and push rearward in a frog-like fashion. Sustained propulsion can be achieved when the kicks are alternated, left leg, then right and so on. The down side to this is that there is no way to keep clean or dry and no one would want to be seen while doing it—this method should only to be used when alone and in a dire situation please.

Eventually we both made it back to the canal—pretty whupped. Everything then had to be washed off completely before it had a chance to dry in the eighty-five degree sun. As we sat there in the water, scrubbing each piece of equipment and clothing repeatedly, we were horrified to find that our shotguns were completely covered in rust—every metal surface, inside and out, and in only one morning! This mud was not right. What chemical or acidic reaction could spawn such results? Afraid for our skins now, it was time to head back to some tap water.

With two more days left in our hunt we were unanimous in our decision not to return to that spot again, nor any spot that looked similar in attributes. Scouting was called for and though we found many spots with suitable numbers of ducks, none seemed quite right—we had become mudaphobics. We did find a fresh water marsh with water deep enough to float the pirogues and containing a fair number of ducks. It was covered with floating water hyacinth, an invasive species that came to the U.S. in the ballast water of ships and now covers just about all fresh water surfaces in the lower delta. It reproduces from seed (which remain viable for up to thirty years) or in a rapid cloning fashion, doubling in size every two weeks in fact, and, so far, all efforts to control it have failed. Even though this marsh did not contain as many birds as other places, we decided to hunt it by splitting up and prowling around in our pirogues—jump shooting style. The day was successful, mud free, and yielded some unique experiences with tippy boats and deeper water, but we missed seeing the large concentrations of birds nearer the coast.

For our final day we chose a spot in the area containing all the mud bays, but on a little, dry, hump of spoil bank that was on a branch canal leading off of one of the larger main canals. The beauty of the choice was that it could be reached by walking on firm, dry, ground. The down side was that there were no ducks using that spot when we found it. The decoys were put out quite close to shore in order to be able to retrieve them with a long pole, and a nice blind was constructed from local vegetation. Our hunt took all morning, kind of slow and steady, a testament to the number of birds in the area—and it was mud-free!

Back in Memphis and basking in the glow of our successful explorer/waterfowler status, we were telling a few of our hunting friends about South Louisiana. Dun made the vehement statement that, "There was not a man alive who could walk in the mud down there", and furthermore, "If you somehow end up stranded a quarter of a mile from dry land, you are a dead man!"

This brought jeers and derision from the uninitiated. Hank Mchorris, a hard-core, hard-charging waterfowler of the Arkansas breed, stated with great conviction that, "There is no mud anywhere worse than we have on the Bayou de View and, I may not like it, but I can walk through any mud anywhere."

Dun and I just looked at each other, silently, and we both started to grin. It doesn't do any good to argue with somebody who is convinced they are right—you have to show them… we were just going to have to go back, with Hank… but that's another story.

William Dunavant Mask— "Big Dun"

The Ten-Degree Rule

Sometimes waterfowling can be at its best when adverse weather conditions are present. In the South, and even way up here in North Dakota where this story is being written, hunters generally blame warm temperatures or a lack of snow cover "up north" for low numbers of waterfowl in their local areas. Most of us eagerly anticipate a forecasted "blue norther" or a spell of sub-freezing temperatures even though the majority of our waterfowl, not all certainly, but most, migrate from their breeding grounds in response to photoperiodic information imprinted in their DNA over eons of evolutionary time. Once along the migrational pathways weather does, obviously, move birds around, but so does hunting pressure, and possibly to an even greater degree.

Most of my early years were spent in the "A" group of waterfowlers who constantly yearned for cold weather—the colder the better. The fact that the ducks all leave an area when the water freezes did not deter my way of thinking. All I wanted was to be there on the big, spectacular migrational days— to endure the elements and battle Mother Nature to a draw.

This can all be very good, wonderful sights are seen and events experienced on those days, but generally, after the big day, everything freezes and the hunting gets a lot less productive.

Productivity is not the only issue affected. Severe cold weather can lead to mishaps, some even catastrophic.

Outboard motors generally have water pumps and I cannot count the number of times that I have witnessed an entire hunt derailed by a frozen one. Sometimes, if unnoticed, this can even ruin the motor—an expensive situation. Fuel lines become brittle as the temperature plummets. Simply brushing against one can make it snap in two, an unwelcome occurrence either at the dock or ten miles downstream. Over time, water will find its way into fuel tanks and bulbs. Though not known to be conducive to the smooth operation of a motor, some can be tolerated, even unnoticed—until it freezes. As the temperature falls, the potential for accidents and malfunctions increases in a far more than proportional correlation.

The dangers are not all mechanical– some can be life threatening. The chance of frostbite on exposed skin increases dramatically with wind speed. At a temperature of zero degrees Fahrenheit with a fifteen mile per hour wind, frost bite can occur in as little as thirty minutes of exposure. Let the wind speed increase to fifty-five miles per hour and

Wind Chill Chart

		Temperature (°F)																
Calm	40	35	30	25	20	15	10	5	0	-5	-10	-15	-20	-25	-30	-35	-40	-45
5	36	31	25	19	13	7	1	-5	-11	-16	-22	-28	-34	-40	-46	-52	-57	-63
10	34	27	21	15	9	3	-4	-10	-16	-22	-28	-35	-41	-47	-53	-59	-66	-72
15	32	25	19	13	6	0	-7	-13	-19	-26	-32	-39	-45	-51	-58	-64	-71	-77
20	30	24	17	11	4	-2	-9	-15	-22	-29	-35	-42	-48	-55	-61	-68	-74	-81
25	29	23	16	9	3	-4	-11	-17	-24	-31	-37	-44	-51	-58	-64	-71	-78	-84
30	28	22	15	8	1	-5	-12	-19	-26	-33	-39	-46	-53	-60	-67	-73	-80	-87
35	28	21	14	7	0	-7	-14	-21	-27	-34	-41	-48	-55	-62	-69	-76	-82	-89
40	27	20	13	6	-1	-8	-15	-22	-29	-36	-43	-50	-57	-64	-71	-78	-84	-91
45	26	19	12	5	-2	-9	-16	-23	-30	-37	-44	-51	-58	-65	-72	-79	-86	-93
50	26	19	12	4	-3	-10	-17	-24	-31	-38	-45	-52	-60	-67	-74	-81	-88	-95
55	25	18	11	4	-3	-11	-18	-25	-32	-39	-46	-54	-61	-68	-75	-82	-89	-97
60	25	17	10	3	-4	-11	-19	-26	-33	-40	-48	-55	-62	-69	-76	-84	-91	-98

Wind (mph)

Frostbite Times 30 minutes 10 minutes 5 minutes

$$\text{Wind Chill (°F)} = 35.74 + 0.6215T - 35.75(V^{0.16}) + 0.4275T(V^{0.16})$$

Where, T= Air Temperature (°F) V= Wind Speed (mph)

Effective 11/01/01

you only have ten minutes. Duck hunters using fast boats can easily encounter these conditions. The preceding chart will help you see what I am talking about.

It is interesting to note that the Inuit Indians, whose ancestors have been fishing in the Arctic for generations, do so bare-handed and do not get frostbitten as easily as the rest of us. Their blood supply is shunted towards the extremities in times of cold-stress, rather than away. This puts them out of the norm, but unless you are an Inuit, it doesn't matter.

Hypothermia can be far worse. If a boat flips over, or someone takes a fall into the water, the body has to try to maintain a normal ninety-eight degree temperature. Involuntary shivering is one method it uses early on in the process, as is the aforementioned constriction of blood vessels leading to the extremities. If the cold-threat is prolonged the body continues to shut down everything else, including the brain, while trying to keep the heart pumping.

In water that is near freezing, the stranded victim of a boating accident that cannot exit the water has less than fifteen minutes before losing consciousness. If your head can remain out of the water you might survive for another thirty. On the night of April fifteenth, 1912, when the Titanic went down, the water temperature in that part of the Atlantic was twenty-eight degrees Fahrenheit. Of the fifteen hundred souls who lost their lives to hypothermia most died within fifteen to thirty minutes depending on what they were wearing and whether or not they had a life jacket on. This next chart will shed more light on this subject.

Hypothermia Table

Thanks to Shawn Baker for submitting this table.

Water Temperature in Degrees F (Degrees C)	Loss of Dexterity (with no protective clothing)	Exhaustion or Unconsciousness	Expected Time of Survival	Recommended Paddling Clothing*
32.5 (0.3)	Under 2 min.	Under 15 min.	Under 15 to 45 min.	Drysuit with fleece layers, neoprene booties, beanie, gloves
32.5 to 40 (0.3 to 4.5)	Under 3 min.	15 to 30 min.	30 to 90 min.	Drysuit with fleece layers, neoprene booties, beanie, gloves
40 to 50 (4.5 to 10)	Under 5 min.	30 to 60 min.	1 to 3 hrs.	Drysuit with fleece or polypro layers, neoprene booties, beanie, gloves
50 to 60 (10 to 15.5)	10 to 15 min.	1 to 2 hrs.	1 to 6 hrs.	Drysuit with polypro layers or wetsuit plus drytop, neoprene booties. hat
60 to 70 (15.5 to 21)	30 to 40 min.	2 to 7 hrs.	2 to 40 hrs.	Wetsuit with light paddling jacket, paddling shoes, hat
70 to 80 (21 to 26.5)	1 to 2 hrs.	2 to 12 hrs.	3 hrs. to indefinite	Thin or shorty wetsuit
Over 80 (Over 26.5)	2 to 12 hrs.	Indefinite	Indefinite	Swimsuit

* This table is intended as a basic guide for paddling apparel selection for various water temperatures. If water/weather conditions are rough or paddlers are inexperienced, clothing one or two levels more protective should be considered. Always wear a PFD.

USK Home Page

25

And so, even though the best day of the season might be missed, I came up with and adhere to, The Ten Degree Rule: If the temperature is ten degrees Fahrenheit or below, I do not go out on big water. Nor do I use an outboard motor in a situation that might leave myself or my companions in trouble. I do not trust anything mechanical when the temperature is that low. It was not always so.

December twenty-third, 1983—five a.m. central time.

The clock over the Planters Bank in Hughes, Arkansas, read negative four degrees Fahrenheit as I passed down the darkened street, boat in tow, on my way to a put-in at Brickies, on the Mississippi River. The wind rocked the truck like a fairground ride and dry leaves, along with occasional pieces of the town's flotsam, skittered across the pavement and through the beams of my headlights. There was not a living thing in sight.

The weathermen had predicted possible single digit temperatures, but not this. It was as cold as I had ever seen, and windy to boot.

I wondered if this was a smart thing to do—macho is only cool when everything goes just right. The river is a dangerous place at any time. Those of us who utilize it accept that fact—and even embrace it, but something in my gut didn't feel just right.

To make myself feel better I resorted to logic. Was I prepared?

The boat that I was pulling was a wide, sixteen-foot semi-vee with high sides. The motor, a thirty-five horse Johnson, was in good shape and the water pump was dry. I had fresh gas and a brand new fuel line. My outfit was well thought out: two toboggan caps, goggles, wool scarf, layers, warm coat, warm boots, and hand warmers in every pocket. My gun had been stripped of all oil– it was completely dry. I had spare gloves in case a pair got wet, spare socks, a thermos of hot coffee, fire starting materials, and food… yet I was uneasy.

A blast of wind pushed the truck over toward the edge of the road and I automatically corrected for the hundredth time, while staring dead ahead, into the cold blackness of night.

This hunt had been arranged via third parties and was going to be with a couple of guys that I had never duck hunted with before. Jack, my usual river hunting partner, was unavailable and he had set me up with a couple of friends from his school.

As I pulled over the levee and through a stand of tall cottonwoods, the headlights showed that my companions were already there. Sensibly, they waited in their vehicle with the engine running and the heater on. Zipping up my coat, I got out to shake hands.

The first to greet me was Bob, with whom I had shot doves a few times. A big, strong, robust fellow, I knew him to be a fabulous wing-shot, good dog-man, and avid duck hunter. Josh, whom I had never met before, struck me as the same sort. It was my guess that anybody who was out here this morning HAD to really love the sport.

Neither of my companions had done much big river hunting before, I was told, but on a day like this it is the only game in town—there just ain't much water at negative four degrees unless it is moving pretty fast.

I looked out over the grey, misty waters from the landing. The river was not very high and a tall bank on the Arkansas side was blocking the gusty, northwest wind– consequently, it was not very choppy. A south wind, on the other hand, would have been out of the question; blowing into the current it would create a huge chop and the resultant spray from our passage would quickly cover the boat in ice. I had seen it happen before, and the weight of the ice keeps building and can eventually cause problems.

My companions were chomping at the bit. I couldn't see anything particularly dangerous and so, just as the rising sun began to brighten the eastern sky, we launched our craft and headed south.

Even riding with the wind at our backs the cold was intense. We took our time, hunkered over and protecting our faces as much as possible. The boat and motor functioned perfectly and we were soon seeing ducks and geese galore!

The weather seemed to have concentrated our whole flyway's supply of waterfowl into the river's channel. Honkers stood on every sand bar and warily watched us go by, not wanting to take off in the blustery wind. Thousands of ducks drifted down stream in huge rafts and, likewise, were reluctant to fly.

I was facing forward, driving, wrapped up like a mummy and with ski goggles on so that I could see ahead. My breath, moving through two over-the-head toboggan caps, formed an ice coating on the outside that blocked the wind. Bob and Josh wisely rode with their backs to the wind and hunched over.

We were coming up on another big raft of ducks and geese and I slowed down and pointed them out—geese being a rare prize in the South. Gloved hands quickly fumbled to load a couple of 870's—and as we coasted nearer to the outer edges of the flock birds erupted in a wall before us and shells flew out of the two guns… but no shots were fired. Firing pins frozen, I guessed, too much oil… we would have to deal with that later. When it is very cold, oil gums up, often keeping a gun from functioning properly. It also collects sand—another reason to shoot a dry gun on the river.

A long strip of sand bar appeared ahead with a nice, calm, eddy behind it. The entire place was literally covered with ducks and geese. This calm oasis was obviously what they were looking for and there was plenty of driftwood scattered about that we could use to build a blind.

I pulled around the bar, into the eddy, and beached the boat right where we needed to hunt in order to unload our gear. All thought of the cold was forgotten as everyone spread out to drag some driftwood back for the blind.

Josh and I headed north; we had our eyes on a couple of large logs that were a couple of hundred yards away. The first one proved heavier than it looked and I turned around to see if Bob would come and help. To my absolute horror I saw that the boat had drifted off from the shore, not too far yet, but it was moving steadily away. Apparently, the wave that washed up when I beached it had frozen instantly, creating an icy slide back into the river. That, our unloading, and the strong wind had been just enough to get it moving.

We started running back, waving our arms and shouting to Bob, who was close to the boat but had not seen the situation yet. When he did, he wasted no time, the gravity of the situation was immediately apparent to all of us.

We were on a flat, sand covered island in the middle of the Mississippi with no cover. The temperature was below zero and the wind was gusting up to thirty miles per hour. That boat was our lifeline, and each of us instantly perceived this.

Bob had on hip boots, as did we all, and waded out to get the boat but couldn't quite reach it—but he was close, sooo close! One long step put him over the top of his boots but the boat was moving away, still, just out of reach! With a big jump he tried to get his upper body over the side. Boots full of water now and muscles stiffening with cold, he didn't make it. The cold water hit him like a stun gun. He couldn't move. I got there next, trying to pull up my boots on the way. The current had him by then and was carrying him parallel to the shore and about twenty yards out. Where I ran into the water my first step was over my boots and the bottom was so steep that my feet went out from under me. I fell over backwards, paddling with my arms back to the bank. Bob had made it to the side of the boat by then and was hanging on, but just barely. The current was swiftly carrying him toward the south end of the bar and it looked like it might be a lot shallower down there. Boots full of water, I lumbered off in that direction trying to get there before Bob passed by. I think Josh was trying to drag a long pole up for Bob to grab, but things were happening too fast for me to notice. Several attempts at different places all ended in deep water and further wettings.

I was now wet to the chest, and arms, and Bob was thoroughly soaked and in shock, about seventy yards away and getting further. The only chance for any of us was for him to get in the boat and drive back to us. We had fire-starting materials in the boat, if we could just get to a bank quickly.

It took a few minutes of yelling but he seemed to snap out of it and tried to pull himself over the side. It was no go; his layer upon layer of clothing was just too heavy. The boat had a drop-down transom and through much coaxing and yelling, issued by those of us on the bank, Bob was able to get mad enough to work his way around to the transom and use the cavitation plate on the motor as a step and drag himself in—SAVED, I thought.

At first he just sat there, hunched over, so cold that he couldn't move. The distance was getting such that communication was difficult in the wind. I doubt if his mind was working properly and he, or we, had only one chance— to get that motor going. Yelling instructions, I guided him through the process that he would normally have been familiar with.

"Put the motor in neutral… there… now pump the bulb… give it a little gas… now, PULL!"

Bob gave it a heave, and nothing happened. I still had not heard him say a single word since he went in the water.

"Pull the choke out… pump the bulb… now PULL!"

Like I said before, Bob is a big guy, and at that moment he was desperate. When he pulled the starter rope this time the recoil spring broke and the entire chord ripped out of the motor and broke. This was a problem that was fixable, but not by somebody in Bob's condition. Next, in a gesture of despair, he slammed his forearm against the front of the motor and broke the entire tiller handle off, flush with the front of the motor. This was not fixable.

Josh and I just stood there for several minutes, the wind blasting our backs, as Bob sat hunched over in the middle of the boat, drifting further and further away, almost out of sight, a dead man– probably before us.

There was nothing further to be done and so we turned away from our friend and started walking north, into the wind, down the long, narrow, strip of sand.

Three-quarters wet, my brain was screaming at me to KEEP MOVING… JUST KEEP MOVING! It was the only thought in my head.

The sand bar went on for quite a way and the two Labradors, Bob's and mine, forged ahead oblivious to the situation. Most of our important gear was in the boat, we didn't have any way to start a fire—as if there was any place to get out of the wind—and we didn't think about bringing a gun—just left them on the sand, and so we walked, not carrying anything. Instead of ending, as we were afraid it would, the bar gradually turned in toward the Mississippi side of the river. Several times we heard shots from somewhere back in the timber… if we could just get to them. When the bar finally ended it was close to the trees, with only about a hundred yards separating us. It was shallow though, and drifting ice had piled up in the shallows and frozen together into a sort of jagged bridge of sorts. We used this bridge and made it to the timber.

Once there we were somewhat out of the wind but not safe. The timber was flooded as far as the eye could see—no telling how deep—and iced-over. To further complicate matters the river had fallen several feet since the original ice had formed and so the ice that we were walking on was suspended, about two to three feet in the air, with water of unknown depth beneath it. Each tree had a cone of ice clenched firmly around it which sagged down into a trough and then back up to the next tree, all suspended in the air. Progress was made by hugging a tree, pushing off for the next, and grabbing it before you slid back down into the trough. Occasionally we broke through, but luckily, each time we were over only a few inches of water.

After about a half-mile of this we came to an old river chute, which blocked our path. The other side was high, dry, ground but the chute was obviously deep and even had open water out in the middle. Hoping the chute would end eventually, we paralleled its course, skating, for another half mile until it became much narrower and finally ice covered.

The ice looked fairly solid and we were getting to be good at judging it. Most of the way there were sticks and saplings that could be used to get back up on the ice if one broke through, but not on the far side. Out there, just before the bank, was a stretch of smooth, deep-water looking ice.

We spread out, as there was a lot of cracking going on. The dogs kept trying to keep near us, as they had been taught, but when they did the ice would sag and make those horrible noises that usually precede catastrophe. When we got to the deep spot it did not look very safe. We sent the dogs on ahead to "hunt dead" on the bank and they made it all right. I gathered two long poles in order to spread my weight out over a much larger area, or to use to rescue myself if need be, and lay down on the ice in a spread eagle fashion with a pole under each hand and made it across without mishap. Josh, seeing my success, chose to take a running start and broke through with one foot, just past the halfway point, fell to his stomach and slid the rest of the way across. Never before had terra firma felt so good.

It was mid-afternoon and we had been traveling on the ice for more than six hours. My legs weren't working well and I knew that I could not stop or I would freeze. We headed in the direction of the shooting we had heard and soon came up with a party of duck hunters who dropped everything to render us aid. We told them about Bob and one of them immediately took off to organize a rescue. Another of the hunters, Mike McDonald, gave me his goose down jumpsuit and socks—for which I will owe him a deep debt of gratitude for the rest of my life. When I peeled off my frozen clothing I noticed that of the three layers of long underwear I was wearing, the outer two were frozen stiff.

It turned out that a deer hunter on the Perry place had seen Bob drifting by, obviously in distress, and had followed him down river quite a way before he could wade out and pull the boat in. He then took Bob straight to the hospital where they warmed him up with, amazingly, no ill effects. Later in the day we met Bob at the hospital and he told us that he had prayed for help... and it had come—"And thank God you had that thermos of hot coffee!" He was not the only one who had done some praying on that day—and all answered also.

Bob's dad drove me back to my vehicle in Arkansas. The sun was shining and the temperature had warmed up a little. It was hard to believe that death had been stalking us all day long.

The next day, Christmas Eve, found me on the Mississippi side looking for my boat. I found it, encased in ice, where the helpful deer hunter had tied it up and with some difficulty it was retrieved. On the day after Christmas, Clayton George volunteered to go back out there with me to retrieve our guns and other gear.

I was a bit ice-shy from the experience, and wore a full wetsuit under my clothes, a habit which I continued with for some time until it was determined that being terminally uncomfortable was not worth it. I then turned to a float coat and lots of wool. After a season of trying to shoot out of a float coat I gave that up also. I now consider it a better idea to tie the boat up really well, and adhere to the ten-degree rule.

As Claybob and I picked our way across the river huge icebergs had made it down from the north and completely barred our passage at times. We used poles, and the bow of the boat, to pry apart bergs and find open passageways that came and went. The weather was much warmer by then and the only scary part was the possibility of getting crushed by moving ice. When we finally arrived at the scene the falling river had stranded a lot of four to six foot thick bergs on top of the bar. Crouching behind these, we quickly shot a limit of canvasbacks and bluebills, the only species left in the area, and did it without putting out a decoy or getting wet—they all fell on the bar. Mysteriously, our party's guns and gear were all absent and never recovered.

I have always felt somewhat at fault for what happened that day, nearly thirty years long past. It was my boat, I was driving, and it was my judgment that put us in that situation. In maritime law, the captain is responsible for the safety of his passengers. He alone ultimately makes all the decisions, and in a bad situation, they need to be the right ones.

Bob and I have remained friendly, in a social fashion, on the rare occasions when our paths have crossed. Neither of us, since that day, has really sought out the other's company nor have we talked about the events of that day other than at the hospital. His grandfather, a great patriarch of the family, apparently implemented his own version of the ten-degree rule. His version seems to have had more to do with who Bob hunted with and where, than anything to do with temperature.

Josh, I have neither seen nor heard from again.

These events all happened many years ago. Young, tough, unmarried, we all thought we were invincible. May you learn from this story a little wisdom, a little discretion, the ten-degree rule, and the power of prayer.

Don't say pirogue to me!

There is an old saying that the difference between men and boys... is the price of their toys. By this marker, waterfowl hunters are the manliest of men. And of all the tools and gadgets used by the intrepid waterfowl hunter, the boat is the most costly. If the preceding assumptions are true, one cannot resist the observation that perhaps any young females that are looking for prospective mates would be wise to look in the side yards of waterfowl hunters homes– just an observation.

There are many different types and sizes of boats used for waterfowl hunting— each designed to function under a particular set of environmental circumstances: flat bottomed boats, usually made of aluminum, are the most common.

They vary widely in size and carrying capacity and seem to do the best job of moving large loads over shallow waters for the least cost. They can be fitted with a semi-vee front and a pointed bow under the misconception that this makes them suitable for rough water. It does not.

V-hull boats do give a better ride in a chop and have a tendency to keep the passengers drier. One sacrifices speed, draft, handling, and load capacity for this ride but gains a safety factor as the v-hulls generally have higher sides also. A true v-bow also aids in navigation through flooded timber because glancing blows to trees do not stop forward progress of the boat.

Canoes need no introduction here and can be used in a variety of applications where not much of a load is being carried, ease of paddling is required, and getting wet is not a life threatening condition.

Propulsion is a part of the cost equation of a boat. Outboard motors can cost thousands of dollars and come in all sorts of sizes and configurations. The standard water-cooled variety is the most common and best way to propel a boat across open water. When extremely shallow conditions, mud, stumps, or vegetation are encountered, the surface drive engines, both long and short shafted are the best choices. Air-cooled and ruggedly built, they can get through with ease what would destroy a standard outboard very quickly. The drawbacks are a loss of speed, maneuverability, noise, and ease of operation.

Airboats, driven by a huge aerial propeller, are in a class by themselves. They can navigate through areas where the craft cannot even float but the drawbacks are huge and their use is usually confined to very specific situations.

To round out the discussion of propulsive methods one must always bear in mind oars, paddles, and sails: sails are rarely used by waterfowlers these days and oars less so with the advent of combustion engines. Paddles are still considered necessary equipment, even with an engine, and will always be so.

There is one more type of boat to consider: not exactly a canoe, though usually pointed at both ends; not exactly a flat-bottom, though quite often flat bottomed—the pirogue.

Pirogues are predominately used in Louisiana. Small, lightweight, easy to carry or put into another boat or vehicle, they are low cost and easy to paddle—if one has the proper technique and decent balance. Not everyone has these requirements, and therein lies our story.

The New Year had blown in with a big rainstorm, followed by ice, and then a frigid forecast for the next ten days or so. Ducks were scarce in the Mid-South and the season was slipping away.

Hank was on sabbatical from his usual haunts around the Bayou De View of Arkansas because of a lack of ducks. This was an unusual situation for him and he was not liking it. He showed up at my door in north Mississippi thinking that all the ducks must be down here, but unfortunately, I had to tell him that we were in the same boat.

"They gotta be somewhere!" was his response when I drove him around to look at my duckless holes.

"They went south," was the only logical reply that I could think of.

"Well, we gotta go after 'em!" says Hank in a passionate display of desperation.

Beginning to catch the enthusiasm I made the observation that: "I bet the coast is covered up right now!"

Wild-eyed, bearded, and wearing the same clothes in the same unwashed condition that I saw him in two weeks ago, Hank was adamant—"Let's go!"

It didn't take us long to pack up, Hank either wears or carries everything he needs at all times during duck season and early the next morning we were on the way to Venice, Louisiana.

Behind the truck, which was piled high with gear, we towed a nineteen foot deep-vee fiberglass boat with a one hundred and thirty horsepower Honda outboard. Inside the big boat and tied securely along both sides of the center console, were two eight foot long pirogues and two double ended kayak paddles. These little craft were made of very thin fiberglass, pointed on both ends, rounded on the bottom, and weighed about thirty pounds apiece. Having hunted the area before, I knew them to be essential equipment.

No one has ever called Hank petit, and he had been eyeing the little craft suspiciously for quite some time. "What are those for? They are way too little to carry anything: no room for enough decoys; too narrow to sit down; they look useless!"

"That's the *ONLY* way to get around down there."

"I might just walk."

Past experiences came flooding back in my mind: incredible mud; no bottom; dogs unable to struggle forward; the tide sucking out all the water in the marsh… "I'm telling you it is like nothing you have ever seen before…"

"We have the worst mud in *The World* at the Bayou," declares Hank, "and I have been walking through it my whole life. There is no mud that I can't walk through!"

Hank is a big, bearded, burly guy, like one of those Duck Dynasty people on TV. If he said that he was going to walk everywhere, that was fine with me. I was going to watch from my pirogue.

We arrived at the Cypress Cove Marina early in the afternoon, got our rooms in the new hotel that had just opened up, and quickly launched the big boat for an exploratory voyage down river. We fully expected to see every duck in America on the marshes along the coast, and for once, we were not disappointed.

Cruising along the bayous and oil field canals one could look out over vast expanses of grassy marsh. Ducks, clouds of ducks, of every shape, size, and color, were present and seemingly in every direction that could be seen. We were like kids in a candy store who couldn't decide what they wanted and our two nickels were the days we had to spend.

After a while, and I could see Hank was getting restless, we passed an unusually large concentration of ducks. "Let's hunt right there!" he exclaimed. It was getting hard for him to stay in the boat.

Something about the situation made me cautious. Something wasn't just right, but I wasn't sure what it was. Taking out my binoculars, things became clear. "Hank, those are pintails out there; the limit is only one on them this year. Man, that is a lot of pintails!"

Hank is an experienced waterfowler and he was convinced—"No, there are a lot of other ducks out there too." Right then, a small group of widgeon came our way and then circled back into the mass—there was going to be no holding Hank back now.

"Ok, ok… we can cross that bay, it looks pretty shallow, and set up on that grassy point." Or, at least that is what I hoped… it still looked like mostly pintails.

We were parked on a canal that was dug by one of the oil companies years ago. Spoil banks on both sides prevented anything but airboat travel from canal to marsh, and besides, most of this marsh was too shallow for propeller driven boats to go. Quickly, we got the pirogues out and over the spoil bank. We loaded a few decoys, some netting, and our guns and shells into the two tiny little craft. My faithful Labrador, Bee, who had done this type of hunt before, carefully laid herself down in the front of mine with her head on her front paws—trying for a low center of gravity. She and I watched as Hank grabbed his bow rope and started out walking. He made it two steps from the spoil bank and sunk down to his waist in only a couple of inches of water. Bubbles rose up all around him as he tried to extricate himself and a black, oily, fluid seeped up from the goo accompanied by a strong sulfurous smell. No progress, forward or back, was exhibited for a few minutes as Bee and I calmly, and with clinical detachment, mentally critiqued his performance. Extraction was enabled by a kind of roll-over-and-crawl technique which Hank performed with only moderate deductions for style. He was now completely covered with mud, beard and gun included, and gasping.

"You ok?" I asked with as much concern as I could muster, while inside my mind was screaming—told you so! It would soon be a moot point though, and I knew it.

"Wow!" was all that he could say for the moment, laying on his back half in the black goo and half on the bank.

"I'm going to see if I can paddle across and get us set up. Sit low in the bottom and come along slow, pushing with your paddle off the bottom. If you tip over don't try to stand up, it is only a few inches deep and you can just sort of roll back in the boat." And with that I headed out to cross the quarter mile of open-looking mostly water.

It turned out to be extremely tough going. The little pirogue drug bottom most of the way requiring hard pulling with the double-ended paddle. It was much easier if one could keep some momentum and that didn't leave any time for looking back to see how Hank was doing.

I made it to the grassy peninsula and glanced back. Hank was still near the far shore, for some reason, but it looked like he had figured it out and was moving. I put out the decoys, just by throwing them, and built our makeshift blind of netting. Ducks were passing by constantly and well within range—mostly pintails and a few redheads. By then he was about halfway and having a little trouble, it looked like. The wind had pushed him over a bit from his original rout and he was actually floating now—for the first time. This seemed like a good thing to me because he could now make much better time, but this was not the case. The pirogue was rapidly rocking from side to side and Hank held the paddle out of the water kind of like a tightrope walker—just before a fall. I saw one side of the boat go down, and then the other. It came to rest on the bottom with some parts of the gunwale still visible, a fact which restored stability, though a wet form of it. A few decoys were floating away but the wind would carry them back to the spoil bank along the canal. With great determination Hank dug in his paddle and resumed forward progress—submarine style. When the water became shallow I saw him bail out with his hat to lighten the load and resume pulling himself along, inch by inch.

It seemed to me that some shooting might spur my partner along—a psychological boost you see. I killed a pintail, a beautiful drake, and a chance redhead. There didn't seem to be any other species around at the moment and so I contented myself with watching Hank negotiate the last hundred yards to semi-solid ground.

A very wise physics professor once told me that, "Without friction, none of us would make it out of this building alive." This statement came to mind as I was watching Hank. The black goo had run down the paddle and onto his hands, arms, and shoulders, the slick, round, bottom of the boat was full of it also, making it difficult to stay seated in one place. I knew what it was like because my boat and body were in a similar state—there was very little friction to be had in that entire parish on that day.

One last patch of floatable water was encountered, ten yards from the bank. The wobble started again, the boat sank, and Hank slid out, gun in hand, and wriggled his exhausted body onto the bank like an old slow alligator on a cold day.

Right then a small flock of pintails zoomed in and hovered over the decoys, not ten yards from the muddy lump on the bank. It was enough to revive the true, waterfowler's spirit. Sitting up, still partly in the water, he used his mud-covered gloves to smear some of the thicker goo off of his beloved old A-5. Finding visibility down the rib inhibited, he tried swishing the gun around in the water for a while. Finally, after looking and blowing down the barrel a few times he was ready to load. I didn't say a word. The ducks continued to pass over our position every few minutes—all pintails. As his receiver closed over the last round I said "… well?"

As the next bunch of pintails was bearing down on us right then, Hank quickly looked in my direction and said, "DON'T EVER SAY PIROGUE TO ME AGAIN!" and with a smooth turn went– "Bang!"—and got his pintail.

We never fired another shot.

Hank is "The Duckman." — just not in a pirogue!

Thank God!

L ike most long-term-afflicted waterfowlers, I don't duck hunt with a lot of different people. I have. At times. But over the years it has become easier, and more comfortable, to stick with a select core group. Often we invite new people to go with us, but it is a gift, in our opinion anyway, and does nothing to change the dynamics of the team.

None of the members of this core group possess any particular "have to" skills. Some can call, some can shoot, and some are wizards at reading ducks and decoy placement. Some just love to be there – as often as possible please. I guess the glue that binds us together has nothing to do with skill at all; it is more likely desire. We all love the sport with a passion.

Occasionally, for varying lengths of time, we have been separated by circumstance. At such times it has been the habit of our membership to assist each other in finding a suitable temporary companion. This is not necessarily an easy task. We all have our physiological foibles and personality disorders and finding the right duck-hunting partner is akin to finding the right wife – they don't grow on trees.

It was that period just after college, about 1983 or so, when everyone is frantically trying to find a place in the world. Much marrying and moving was going on in my age group, as well as the usual floundering around in the work force in order to find jobs that would support us in the manner that we wished to become accustomed to. It is at this time in life that one really becomes in awe of one's parents. They did it – and the odds seem insurmountable.

I had been hunting the Mississippi River, by myself, quite a bit. It is the most dangerous venue we have in our part of the world, and a companion lessons the degree of risk by half – at least. Steep put-in places, the potential of falling out of the boat, picking up decoys in swift current, getting the boat beached or stuck between trees, are all everyday type occurrences on the mighty Mississippi. For this kind of hunting not just anybody will do. Experience is a great asset, as is calm in the face of a crisis. It has to be someone who can read a situation and come up with an innovative solution. But mostly, it has to be someone who appreciates the solitude on the big river and accepts the danger as part of it.

I had been scouting for a couple of days south of Memphis and located an excellent prospect. Mallards, several thousand in all, were dry-feeding in some big bean fields on the Arkansas side and making a short flight to the river for water and gravel. They came in tens and twenties, for the most part, and from about nine o'clock in the morning until well into the afternoon. The kicker was that where they were using was a big cove off of a sand bar, without a twig or blade of grass on it. On the south side of the cove, the sand bar changed elevation from flat to about ten feet above the current water level. It was in my mind to dig a pit up on top of that hill, perfectly level with the sand around it, and place a big spread of decoys in the eddy below. The sun would be mostly at my back and in the ducks eyes, the eddying currents would give the decoys lifelike motion, and even a north wind would give the ducks a trouble free approach over the featureless sandy plain. It was going to be great, and even if the water level came up it could probably be used for several days – a rare scenario on the big river.

The sand was brownish-white, fine-textured up on the hill, and loose – easy enough to dig a hole, but not a nice, clean, steep-sided one. What was needed was a narrow pit. One that a person could hunker down in and be invisible to the ducks, unless, of course, they were directly overhead.

On the drive home from scouting my mind was busy with the possible options available. Past experience had taught me that to dig a hole four feet deep in dry sand, one ended up with a crater twenty feet wide. Why not build a plywood box with no bottom or top, carry it out there in the boat, set it down right where the pit needed to be, and get inside and start digging. If one threw all the sand outside the box, it would gradually go down as the outside built up. Presto! We have a nice, steep sided, well hidden, duck shooting pit.

This was obviously going to take a little work, and there were some glossed-over logistical issues, but I was on a roll. All that was needed was a stout partner, the pit, and two shovels.

The box didn't take too long. Eight feet long, four feet tall, and three feet wide, it was a masterpiece of scrap lumber. It even had a little bench that could be added after the digging was all done and a brace for the middle so that hopefully the weight of the sand wouldn't crush the sides before it was complete.

I had called John Stokes— river hunter extraordinaire and mentor in these matters— to honor him with an invitation to participate in this historic endeavor. Past experience had proven him to be an excellent digger and appreciative of truly innovative set-up techniques, but he said, rather quickly, that he had other engagements. It may have been that age was starting to endow him with some new degree of intuition – I'm not sure – but he did tell me, after some reflection, to call up Bobby Cox, as he would be the perfect candidate for this sort of expedition.

Mr. Cox was an old crony of John's and a veteran river hunter. Known to be a bit quirky, and a definite loner, he almost never hunted with anyone else. He also never used a duck call, instead relying on a legendary ability to place and tweak a decoy spread until the ducks did exactly what he wanted them to. The chance to learn from one of the great river sages was a rare and wonderful opportunity and so I gave him a call.

He answered the phone on the first ring, which surprised me. A big time lawyer, instrumental in the start up of Fed-X, I expected to wade through a few secretaries with an eventual call back option. I got right to the point: told him the set up, gave him my idea, and asked him what he thought.

"Nine o'clock you say? Meet me at my house at seven. Oh, and I'll bring lunch."

That was easy enough; it was time to get loaded.

After the sixteen foot, high-sided riverboat was checked and gassed-up, the decoys were then loaded in such a way that the pit could be placed in the middle. It weighed a bit more than I thought and it was a struggle to get it in there –

no matter, we had two of us to get it out. The four-foot height didn't look so big on the ground, but sitting in the boat it looked like I was carrying a house. A strap was found, the kind with a ratchet style buckle, and a couple of extra ropes to secure it. This thing was really going to catch some wind, I thought, as I looked proudly at my handiwork one last time before going in for the night.

My arrival at Mr. Cox's house was timed promptly at six forty-five according to the unwritten rule of duck hunters to be at least fifteen minutes early for any expedition. He was ready and waiting, outside, with his old double gun, bag, and thermos. At first he just stood there . . . not saying a thing. His eyes seemed to be fixed on the boat. The silence began to get a little awkward and so I started to explain how it was all going to work perfectly because I had it all figured out. We drove down the street and got on to the expressway as I went into great detail about how, as we both stood in the middle and threw the sand out, gravity and our slight contribution of labor, would enable the box to slowly go down with us. Gathering speed, both with the truck and my subject, I went into more detail about how we could get it up the hill and . . . there was a tremendous cracking sound. We both looked toward the rear and saw the gigantic box air-born, over the pavement. It somersaulted end-over-end twice in the air, seemingly in slow motion, before slamming into the pavement at seventy miles per hour. Within a second, my entire hopes and dreams were dashed into a thousand pieces, not one of which was bigger than my hand. I slowed down a little, just to see if there was anything to salvage. Not a chance, there was nothing to be done. As I sped back up, not even looking in the rearview mirror, Mr. Cox finally turned back around and said what I believe were his first words of the trip – "THANK GOD!"

L-R Bobby Cox and long-time friend and hunting partner,
Dr. Sid Wilroy

Last Days

Most true hunters arrange their entire lives around hunting season. Vacations are heavily weighted towards the proper time of year; social engagements are neglected, or at least grudgingly participated in during "the season", and many people only see their best and most valued friends during this time. It is this year-round focus that makes last days so special.

Almost all turkey hunters are going to at least go out and listen on the last day. It matters not that by then the vegetation is so thick you probably couldn't hear a turkey at a hundred yards –if there were any still gobbling—one just has to go.

Deer hunters in the northern states have only a short window to fill their tags and most go every day they can. But in the southern states, deer season goes on forever: October through February in some cases, and all the truly avid deer hunters are out there on the last day. It doesn't matter that the bucks are already losing their antlers and the does are thin and skittish –one just has to go, even if you have no intention of shooting anything.

Duck hunters are, if anything, even more passionate. The year-round fervent longing for duck season to open back up leaves one with almost a fear of it closing again. Last days, for the true waterfowler, are usually hallowed, ritualized occasions; a time of reflection, wishes for the birds safe passage to northern breeding grounds and a speedy return next year.

Mississippi has, for many years, chosen the latest closing date possible for waterfowl seasons –January thirty-first. Some years the northern part of the state is all iced-up and the ducks are down on the coast. Other years it can be too warm and all the ducks might be further north. It doesn't matter because the season is open and we all have to go. In fact, due to our late closing date, people pour in from all over the country; possibly because they missed their own last day and had to come try ours –I don't know, but they do show up.

These people have strange boats and even stranger ways of doing things. They may come from hundreds of miles away and bring their own area's customs and moralities, or lack thereof, with them. Herein lies the problem: every federal warden in the country worth the ink in his pen is here with them. Like bears to a salmon run they go where the pickings are best, and Mississippi, on the last weekend, is the only pool left with any fish.

Clay, a long-time bow hunting companion and one of the most knowledgeable people on any subject concerning big deer, turkeys, or anything else in the woods for that matter, was taking a rare sabbatical. A sabbatical from the woods that is— he wanted to go duck hunting. I was, and still seem to be, an easily manipulated person in these matters.

We had a wonderful hunt that morning, the last of the 1990 season. Moon Lake was skimmed-over with ice except for the mouth of Phillips Bayou, and a convenient grove of cypress trees afforded perfect cover to shoot from. We were done early and the mallards continued to pour into the hole while we just sat back and watched. The bright sunshine, coming from a cold, deep blue sky, lit up the ducks' colors as stiff-winged flights made slow, gliding approaches into a steady fifteen mile an hour north wind.

Years ago, Moon Lake was a bend of the mighty Mississippi River. At some point in time, as rivers do, a new channel was cut and Moon Lake was left isolated, for most of the year, from the main river. In 1811 the US Army Corps of Engineers built the Great Levee and supposedly isolated Moon Lake from its parent river for all time. The levee, though big and tall, does not affect duck travel. They still fly the old pathways and migrational patterns set down eons ago, and that is what they were doing for us.

My wife, Pumpkin, would love to see this, I thought, as we marveled at the winged spectacle taking place before us. We were hunting only five minutes by boat from my house, if one drove really fast, and so we left the decoys out and ran back up the lake to get her.

Now Pumpkin is not the fastest person in the world to get ready. Usually it takes an hour to get ready to get ready; consequently it was about two o'clock in the afternoon when we headed back out on the lake. Our broken ice trail had re-frozen in places but once near the moving water at the mouth of the bayou everything was still open.

There were a lot of ducks on the water and a good many in the air. It was decided to take a quick run up the bayou itself, just to see what was up there, and we found the winding bayou to have a clear channel down the middle with fairly thick ice on the edges. We were jumping quite a few ducks around every bend, and I found that by going fast, and really judging the slide of the flat-bottomed boat perfectly, I could put the boat right underneath the ducks –sometimes only an arm's length away. This was a lot of fun for a few sharp bends until I slid the boat a little too far on one turn and hit some thick ice, which dramatically changed our course – but not Clay's. He continued on the original course, for some reason, and then decided to take up ice skating, on his back—another poor choice on his part because the ice was not thick enough to hold him. The water being very deep at that time, I assumed he would want to get back in and was in the process of maneuvering to expedite this process when Clay, due to unknown physical processes, landed back in the bottom of the boat. I guess the water was unpleasant.

We took Clay back to the house and there are only two choices in a situation like this: fast or slow. I was poking along, using the slow method, while Clay turned blue, until he finally said, "Let's get it over with," and we did.

A quick change into dry clothes and we were all three back on the water with only a couple of hours left in the season.

Pumpkin had two boxes of shells and the only gun in the boat. The ducks were decoying in large bunches; the little twenty gauge Citori would go pop-pop and the ducks would leave, usually all of them, and a few minutes later another bunch would do the same thing. She wanted all greenheads, and eventually got them, but the amount, and steady nature of the shooting had attracted attention.

Unbeknownst to us, a couple of federal wardens had been attracted by the smell of blood. Putting their boat in a couple of miles away in an area of wind opened water, they had then cautiously crept down the edge of the lake— going from tree to tree in approved game warden fashion— until stopped by ice. Knowing that we would hear them coming if they ventured any further, the choice had been made to spy on us from a half mile away with their state of the art optics and telephoto lenses.

Alas, all that they could see were the large clouds of ducks dipping below the tree line and then hear the two shots, again and again and again.

Wardens are taught to count shots, estimate percentages, and distrust in general. Back-up was soon called in and ink pens warmed up for the coming volume of work.

Meanwhile our shooter killed her last greenhead and we had to dig around in the bottom of the boat to find a shell for her to do it with.

Legal shooting time ended as we picked up the decoys, taking our time, savoring the last motions of a wonderful season for which we were truly thankful. Motoring back was equally stress-free with no worries or the contemplation of any such; the wind had laid down and the lake and sky seemed to come together into an all-encompassing portrait as we slowly coasted back to the pier.

Suddenly, seemingly out of nowhere, a massive craft roared alongside, smashing ice and sending shards scattering for hundreds of feet to the sides as it came. Lights blazed into our eyes and with powerful engines throbbing a loud voice told us not to move: "Federal wardens: keep your hands in plain sight and step away from the boat!" We were immediately separated and asked to produce licenses –Pumpkin proudly displayed hers, with a signed duck stamp and a very fine limit of greenheads!

"Mr. Neely, may I see your license?"

"I don't have one with me, I wasn't hunting."

This perplexed my interrogator and I could tell he did not believe me. With a sly look, he then asked, "I need to check your shells then."

"My wife shot them all."

This was not going as planned, I could tell –"All of them?"

"All."

It was as if he had a list of questions but was not listening to the answers; "Let me check your gun then please."

"Don't have one," I told him, all the while trying very hard to remain polite, "I've got a license and a gun in the house if you would like to check them, but not with me."

"Mr. Neely, just what were you doing out there?"

"I took my wife out to close the season. Clay and I went this morning and we got our limits."

As if lecturing to a child, the warden said, "You are supposed to keep your license on your person at all times while engaged in the act of hunting or fishing."

"Yes, but I wasn't hunting, she was." By this time I was starting to get a little angry –standing on my own pier and trying to be nice while getting the third degree. I could hear Clay, and he was getting the same questions and giving the same answers, and it didn't seem to be helping any.

The older, more experienced of the two wardens was now poking around in our boat. He chuckled a little, at what I couldn't tell, and then said, "Their telling the truth, there is only one gun and a whole bunch of twenty gauge steel hulls, all empty."

At this everyone started to relax and the wardens gave up on trying to write us a ticket. We apologized for wasting their time and they said no problem, they had done well over the weekend. It was their opinion that Mississippi was the best of all places for them because the stuff they saw going on down here was like nowhere else in the country.

"We come down here every year, on the last weekend, and find people doing the craziest stuff: flagrant violations of shooting hours, limits, licenses—you name it, we see it all and then some; it's like Christmas for us!"

Bidding the gentlemen goodbye, we got back to the unloading and putting up of gear for another year.

Those two were from the Chesapeake Bay area and were real sticklers for dotted I's and crossed T's. I hope that they don't get so caught up in the rules that they scare people away from the sport. Without duck hunters, there would soon be no ducks; I would bet that we pay for 99% of all the conservation work actually accomplished on this continent. Game wardening is a tough and important job, but to be a good one takes a lot of savvy and common sense, along with compassion –both for the wildlife and the people who love to pursue them.

Their comment on Southerners' ethics caused me some reflection. As already mentioned, most of the flagrant violations that I see, these days at least, come from this influx of out-of-staters who don't have a proper reverence for the traditions of the sport –and especially last day's traditions. Year after year I have heard a group pounding away thirty minutes or more after sunset on the last day – a time when the ducks should have been completely safe for another year. I cannot be the one to cast the first stone in a situation like this, but it saddens me. Discrete telephone calls have been made to people who know the perpetrators. Maybe that will help.

As for the bad reputation we have –alluded to by the federal agents – let's just blame it on the Yankees . . .or not.

Zoda

Ted, or Zoda as he was commonly referred to in high school, was two grades above me and light years ahead in life's more earthy experiences. With a prominent head of bright red and unkempt hair, exuberant social skills and boundless energy, he was into just about anything that a young man could be at his age and demographic station. An exceptionally keen minded individual, he once told me that he considered himself an oratoriador in the old style tradition and that he could talk himself into, and out of, any situation that might arise.

Above all else, his passion was hunting. Having no money, no car, and no land of his own did not deter him in the least—his orative powers got him onto many of the best duck and turkey places in the South. When these failed him he would convince a buddy to drive him out and knock on a few doors, invariably gaining some sort of permission and quite often a new and lasting acquaintance.

Our high school, Memphis University School, prided itself on preparing young men for college and the world beyond. Time was regimented, deadlines strict, and dress codes enforced. Occasionally, course schedules left one with a free period at a certain time of the day. Though ostensibly these periods were to prepare one's self for the day's challenges, they were not always used in such a manner.

Ted was practicing his turkey calling on the day that I met him. He had a penchant for any type of call and in fact had won the Mid-South duck calling championship that very year. I was aware of this because our principal had acknowledged the feat in chapel and called upon Ted to give an unabashed exhibition—which he performed flawlessly—with an old wooden call made by P.S. Olt– A call not many can blow because it takes a tremendous amount of air. So here he was, yelping and clucking away at school. I was drawn to the sounds as a moth to flame.

I came over to see how he was doing it, as he had no visible contraption to make the noise, and he promptly pulled another mouth call out of his pocket and said, "Wash it off in the water fountain and give it a try."

I did, and only managed some strange hissing noises at first. He coached me, patiently explaining each type of call and how to make it. Soon I was yelping away on an M.L. Lynch diaphragm call and attempting a few clucks.

Having read about turkey hunting, I was enamored with the idea of matching wits with the supernaturally suspicious wild turkey gobbler, but had never actually seen or heard one. When Ted heard this, he immediately stated that he could show me one this Friday afternoon, if I had wheels. That was on a Monday and we were good to go.

Before the sun set on that very day I was the proud owner of my own Lynch diaphragm call and practice started in earnest. Our school lounge rang with the sounds of wild turkeys all the next week. Another student, Bayard Erb, surprised us by bringing a box call, also made by M.L. Lynch, and joined in the practice sessions exhibiting a degree of skill far surpassing either Ted or me. The three of us had a great time practicing and both Bayard and Ted swapped stories of failure and success that kept me captivated.

When Friday rolled around we were out the door before the bell quit ringing. Ted hopped in the already running truck and said, "Head north, towards Shelby Forest," and proceeded to guide me through the slums and back ways of North Memphis. He used side roads and alleyways most of the time, and avoided main roads and highways. It all seemed surprisingly familiar to him and the reason for this, which later became apparent, was that he was never in possession of a valid driver's license for very long. It was a legal obstacle that altered his perception of how to get from point A to point B.

Eventually we left the city and got into farm country. At a sharecroppers house Ted hopped out, had a word with an older colored gentleman, jumped back in and said, "We're good." We then drove down the road a little piece, turned into a field at a Benjestown Road sign, and parked at a small patch of woods.

Standing outside the truck Ted's demeanor had changed to all business. "No talking when we enter the woods," he explained. "I'll point out turkey sign, if there is any, and then we will sit down and try to call up a turkey. Once we sit down don't move. Got it?"

Getting worried I asked "How long will we sit?"

"As long as it takes," he said with a grin, "And, by the way, these tracks right at our feet are fresh."

I was startled to look down and see turkey tracks, real ones, and they did look fresh.

After hacking and coughing at the truck for a minute or two—in order to get it over with he explained—Ted started out at a rapid pace for a short-legged chain smoker. Or, at least it seemed that way to me. Staying right behind him, as instructed, and trying to move as quietly as possible, I looked and nodded as he pointed out occasional scratch marks and feathers. Ted moved like a ghost in the woods and I struggled to make as little noise as he. Soon we came to a cane thicket and he stopped to make a call before trying to cross it. I didn't hear anything but he immediately sank to the ground motioning for me to follow suit, and quickly. He gave another series of yelps and was answered immediately, this time from close by.

"He's coming," whispered Ted, "Get down and don't move!"

I was already sitting on the ground and so I just rolled over flat on my stomach. A few seconds later there was a faint crackling of leaves followed by a soundless pause… a loud "PUTT!" and then the thunderous roar of great wings.

In an excited whisper Ted was asking, "What did you think of that?"

I had to admit that it was the most exciting thing I had ever done, "and can we hunt here next weekend when the season opens?"

"Yeah sure," he said, "but wasn't he something! I mean beautiful—standing in that patch of sunlight."

"Uh… well… I didn't actually see him. I was so scared that I might frighten him off that I was lying down… with my face in the dirt—but I heard him!" Now I really wanted to call one up myself, and, hopefully, get to see him!

Like a good coach, Ted stayed positive, "You sound great on that call and you'll see one next weekend."

Another week of practice and anticipation went by and then Saturday morning found us in the woods in a driving rainstorm. Ted sent me one way and he went another. This may seem odd, due to my inexperience, but it is the way I wanted it. He did offer to call for me but this was something that I wanted to do myself. There is nothing more exciting than learning the ropes of a new game; learning how to hunt a new species or fish a new lake, and besides, in my mind turkey hunting is a solitary sport—mano a mano; just your wits against an old gobblers cunning. If I ever did shoot one it was going to mean a lot to me.

I set up with my back against the bole of a large oak tree. Calling every few minutes, my senses were on red alert. It seemed as if every nerve ending in my body was sticking out at least a quarter of an inch—like antennae. It sounded like there were turkeys everywhere—I didn't know that a certain type of blackbird called a purple grackle gobbles in the spring, or that a possum can create a perfect imitation of a whole flock of turkeys walking through the leaves. My heart raced the entire morning as every creature in the woods did their best to imitate turkey sounds.

Sometime later the rain stopped and an occasional feeble ray of sunshine would briefly break through a grey and overcast sky. Suddenly, two shots broke the stillness, silencing all the forest denizens and a huge, black, bird came sailing across the treetops and lit on a limb directly in front of me and about fifty yards away. I couldn't move a muscle as the turkey craned his neck back and forth, looking for danger. I was fairly certain that this was a gobbler, but I wasn't about to shoot until a better look presented itself.

Thirty minutes later it appeared that the big bird had settled down a bit and I decided to try a little calling. My yelps were better than my clucks, or so I thought, and so I gave three soft ones without moving anything other than my jaw.

The bird gave a low "…Cluck?"

Encouraged, I gave him back the same low "…Cluck?"

It seemed like we were communicating. I waited a few minutes and repeated the same soft yelps… Mr. Tom's head shot up and with a loud "PUTT!", he went airborne in a thunderous rush of wing power, followed by an even louder "BOOM"… of a shotgun. For the first time in quite a while I looked down at the ground, and there was Ted, standing on my turkey's neck.

"Wow, I didn't know you were there!" says he, "Why didn't you shoot?"

"I was trying to call him down—they always gobble in all the stories you guys tell," was my sheepish reply.

Ted patiently continued my education that spring. We hunted several places, morning and evening, school days and weekends, good weather or bad. I had never done anything that required that much commitment and focus—it was an addiction, and we both had it to a very high degree.

I began to fall asleep at school, and in the woods also. Grades, heretofore never a top priority for me, began to suffer. My parents were not pleased… I had to get a turkey soon!

The places we hunted had a few turkeys in them, at times, but never many and they seemed to move in and out of our reach. For almost the whole of my first year as a turkey hunter I hunted strictly on sign. I never heard a turkey gobble. It was all cold-calling and set up and wait. Every now and then I would call up a hen and my whole body would shake uncontrollably afterwards. Having never experienced it any other way, I was not disheartened. I figured that one day, if I kept going often enough, one would have to trip over a log and break his neck right in front of me—it was simply the law of averages.

Towards the end of the season I was out scouting some new territory one Thursday afternoon. A dirt bike track outside of West Memphis wound its way through some river bottom woods and I had permission to hunt there—"just don't get run over." Ted was off on some other adventure and I was alone. Carefully easing along the bike track, which was great because the soft chewed-up dirt was really quiet to walk on, I would stop and call every few minutes and usually wait a few more before moving on. At the third or fourth stop, not very far along really, I put my hands up to my mouth and gave a loud, questioning, "Cluck?" Immediately a turkey clucked back and walked into view. It was a gobbler– a big one. I froze, never thinking of taking a shot until he had walked off. He might have been a little spooked, but not terribly. I determined not to call anymore and not to move until dark came and I could get out without being detected. The turkey flew up to roost, a good ways off but within hearing, and I took careful landmarks that could be found in the darkness and left, believing that tomorrow was the day.

School bells rang at eight A.M. and one was considered late at eight-ten. Sunrise was at six-thirty and I was going to be forty minutes from school, if I was lucky. It was a tight window; I would have to be in my truck and headed out by seven-thirty. Just an average day for a turkey hunter, I thought.

I was there extra early the next morning, face painted and full camo, in position by five-thirty. The turkey gobbled, on cue, at six o'clock when I made my first yelp. We kept up a dialogue for a while and I could actually see him, in his tree, when he gobbled. When he left the limb it was in the other direction and I gave a desperate cackle that appeared to turn him around in mid-air. When he lit it could not have been more than thirty yards away but I could not see him. I had made the neophyte mistake of setting up with a small ridge between us, and, if he came over the top, our first glimpse of each other was going to be eye to eye. I grabbed my gun and rolled onto my stomach, thinking that I would wriggle to the top and shoot. Indecision, or intuition, caused me to freeze where I was and as my brain tried to process all the variables and come up with a best-case scenario, the grass next to me started to move and the gobbler appeared, three feet away, head low to the ground and sneaking. It was no longer a tactical problem; it was time to do something.

At the first minute tensing of muscle, before even starting up from the ground, he flushed like a quail—a really big, really fast, quail. Adrenaline, that substance which causes so many miraculous effects on our bodies, apparently is deleterious in some doses and some situations. No one in the history of mankind has ever taken as long as I did to get to my knees, mount the gun, and take a shot. Believe it or not, I only had time for one, but it was enough.

The bell rang two minutes before I slid into my seat; it was the third strike for me and earned me a Saturday school. I didn't care; it was the biggest day of my life. Ted was all congratulations as I told him all about my hunt and showed him the turkey at lunchtime. Both he and I showed the turkey to anyone who would come out and look all during the day and at a party that night. It may have been a little silly, but we kept it up until the wee hours. I think he was as proud of that turkey as I was, and, rightfully so I might add.

During the course of the evening's festivities I mentioned to him that I had earned my first Saturday school. I was a bit worried about it because the teacher in charge had a reputation for being tough on students in that situation. Ted, who had a vast amount of experience in these matters said, "No problem, the guy wants to learn how to turkey call so take your call with you and help him out. I'll put in a good word for you."

True to his word, Ted paved the way for me and I spent the entire morning calling turkeys and actually got to be good friends with the teacher—a fact that would come in handy in future turkey seasons.

Days turned into weeks and months to years. Ted and I had many great adventures in pursuit of ducks, turkeys, doves, and fish. No amount of effort was too great an expenditure for him. He could always be counted upon to go—even when conditions were not good. He might wear the same set of clothes for an entire week, or skip several nights sleep, but he was always there the next morning; maybe a bit bleary-eyed, but there.

Sometimes our paths parted for a while but we stayed in touch over the years, and so it came to be that after a long absence, an afternoon adventure was called for.

The day was bright and clear, even hot, but not unusually so for Memphis in September. We decided to just go take a ride on the Mississippi River—guns along of course—just to catch up and enjoy getting out of the city. Our official story was that we were going dove hunting, but the chance of shooting anything more than a dove or two on the mile wide river while riding around in a boat, was pretty slim.

As usual I had my Labrador retriever along, Lady, and a bucket of reloads. It's not that I anticipated a need for a hundred rounds of ammunition, that's just what was in the bucket when I grabbed it. Ted had a box of shells... half full. This was not an unusual situation for him. Having many and varied interests competing for financing—some legal, others not—Ted quite often overestimated his shooting skill, or underestimated his need for ammo. However you wish to put it, he ran out of shells all the time. Nevertheless, if we shot more than a box apiece on this trip I would be surprised. Though known for being extremely stingy with my equipment, I chose not to say anything—thinking that at most, I would have to *lend* him a couple of handfuls.

We motored north, under the bridge and up the Tennessee bank, and then cut across to check the sand bars around Dacus Lake. The sun beat down with a vengeance and no birds were in evidence probably because we were a bit early in the day to catch them coming to water. Heading back north again, we had just passed the Hickman Bar when I saw a couple of birds sail down, way out in the middle of the sand bar, and disappear. The bar was dirty-white, pancake-flat, and featureless—maybe a quarter of a mile across—and I couldn't see any reason why those birds went down out there. We decided that the best course of action was to wait and watch.

Across the bar, on the Tennessee side and atop a sixty-foot high, eroded bluff, a solid wood line presented itself—solid, except for one large gap. Several hundred yards wide, this gap appeared to lead back inland for a long way—possibly a pipeline right of way. Over the next few minutes several small groups of doves came through this gap flying extremely high—as if from a great distance—and then set their wings and spiraled down towards the middle of this sand bar, several hundred feet below.

It was ninety-five degrees outside, probably one hundred and fifteen out on the sand, and not even a dead twig to provide shade out there. We stripped off all nonessential clothing, jumped in the river to get wet, grabbed our guns and ammunition and headed out.

A ten minute trudge in sand, some loose and some packed, all shimmering with heat waves, brought us to a small depression full of cool-clear water that welled up from deeper sands below. A few doves got up from the bank, too far away to shoot, as we took up positions on one side of this pond. Squinting into the blazing sun, we looked at each other and laughed at our predicament: the sand bar was as flat as a concrete slab, the water hole was only about ten feet across, and we stuck out like two Egyptian pyramids in the middle of the dessert.

And then they started to come. From so high and so far away that they looked like specks, they came. In two's, three's, ten's and twenty's they came. At first, we shot them as soon as they got low enough; later, we learned that they would come right to the water and could be shot like ducks—hovering over decoys. We moved closer together for communication purposes and shot as a team—each taking the outside birds on his side and working toward the middle. Lady was overwhelmed. No virgin at a fast dove shoot, she had never quit on me before. She left us and went back to the river and laid down in the water—it probably saved her life.

As our guns grew hotter they burned our fingers—but the pace just quickened. I noticed Ted was only shooting one time at each group. While loading as fast as possible I asked him, "Is your gun messing up?"

"No, I'm out—shooting yours now! I'm only getting one at a time though!"

"Git some more!" I yelled, "This can't last much longer!"

But it did. Long before the birds quit we were out of ammo; beet red, sunburned, with blistered hands and ringing ears–but happy.

By the time we got back to the boat I was no longer mad at Lady. She scraped and hunkered her apology for a minute or two, and then as dogs do, moved quickly on to happy. We swam in the cool river water, took some pictures, and drank an ice-cold beer before heading back to town—maybe the best beer I ever had. With the setting sun, the river a glassy calm, after the day we had just experienced, it is a memory that will be with us for all the rest of our days. At that time we did not know that this would be the last time we ever shot doves together. Even if we had, it would not have made it any more memorable.

Shortly thereafter Ted took a job with a big cotton company. Soon he was wheeling and dealing in the international market and found himself stationed in Australia. It happened something like this: a bit too much to drink; a long sandy road way out in the outback; a devastating crash—Ted has been a quadriplegic these last twenty-three years.

With the advent of the technological age and the help of a number of friends, Ted has never had to give up his interest in the blood sports. He now rules an information empire, via the Internet and voice recognition technology, whereby he is in constant contact with hunters and fishermen the world over. He knows where the fish are biting, where the duck migration is, and in what areas the turkeys are starting to "get right." He can be trusted with confidentiality but if it is not necessary, don't shackle him with that responsibility–information is the currency of his lifestyle. If you find him, over the Internet, you will have a trusted friend forever—I hope you do, so that he won't send me so many junk e-mails!

The author and Zoda

Cedar Grove road

The pursuit of turkeys, male turkeys, in the spring, is not something that can be classified by a single word. Certainly not by the term "sport", or "recreation", or any other word that invokes a relaxing or trivial way to spend one's time. "Hunt" comes a little closer but only when used in a focused, passionate, determined manner. A dove hunt can be fun; a foxhunt can be exuberant; a turkey hunt is serious business.

For many years I have hunted turkeys on most mornings of the spring season. I don't kill a turkey every time I go and I don't want to. Some years, when the turkey crop is low, I'll only take a bird or two –but I still have to get up every morning before daylight, just to be there. I can't stand the thought of missing out on those mornings when the big toms really open up. The age old question about why turkeys gobble some mornings and not others is something I wish to answer –and why they move leks, or bunch up and then spread back out a few days later –or come to a call with abandon one day when the same tom would not take one step toward you the last ten days in a row.

These questions and a million others are all part of the term "hunt." We hunt not just for the kill, but for knowledge, answers, and the more one has to learn the more gratifying are the days afield.

Turkey season was months away when I signed up for a continuing education course offered by my alma mater, Mississippi State University. The title for the course was "Managing Timber on Private Lands in Mississippi." As a farmer, and farm manager with some timber to look after, it seemed like a worthwhile endeavor. I knew something about growing crops, and a little about managing timber for wildlife, but my knowledge of timber for money was woefully inadequate.

The course was a three-day affair, April fifth, sixth, and seventh –right in the middle of prime-time turkey season. Our season opens about the middle of March and runs through April. On a normal year the turkeys start gobbling in mid-March and one can have about two weeks of some of the finest hunting weather you could ask for – no mosquitoes, cold mornings, and very little green vegetation to block sound. My plan, then, was to get as much hunting in as possible early and take a few days off for the course. But, as so often happens with the plans of men, it was not a normal year.

By the time April first arrived I had yet to hear a single gobble. Persistent cold, wet, weather had settled on the Delta in February and never let up. Now I know that the biologists tell us that photoperiodism triggers the hormonal changes that initiate the breeding cycle in wild turkeys. That it is increasing day length that does it –but the turkeys don't know it. To them it was still winter, and cold, and wet.

Mississippi State University, located in Starkville, is over a hundred miles south of my farm. South, as in where it is warmer. There are numerous state-owned, county-owned, school-owned, and nationally-owned public lands around there that one can legally hunt on. At one time I calculated something in the vicinity of a million acres –depending upon how far you wish to travel. Furthermore, I spent four years down there turkey hunting, bow hunting, trapping, and not going to class. I decided to take my gun and camouflage along— just in case.

The course schedule started at eight a.m. and so on the first morning I did a quick, "daylight" road survey about thirty minutes from campus. Drive a quarter of a mile and get out and hoot like an owl. Listen. Repeat. I located two toms and triangulated their positions as best I could. One looked easier to get to and was chosen for day two –and it was going to have to be early and quick.

Scouting chores over, I was back in time for class. Anything having to do with timber, farming, or wildlife I find fascinating, and this was no exception. The course was geared towards pine production –the biggest industry in the state – with some segments pertaining to bottomland hardwood. The first speaker on day two was to be a pine guy. One thing you won't find along the Mississippi River delta bottomland is pine trees and so this gave me an extra hour in the morning, for which I was grateful –few turkeys I have ever met operate on a schedule.

Two of the rules for hunting on public land are to get there early and park your truck conspicuously –I did both that morning. Another universal truth is that you don't blunder into a suspected gobblers roosting area until he has given his exact location away. I did it this time, and got away with it.

I had been sitting still, on the ground, for thirty minutes without making a sound when he gobbled for the first time. He was right where he should have been, a miracle in itself, and twenty minutes later, when it was almost light enough to shoot, I gave a few soft "tree" calls. He answered immediately, which prompted me to make my first mistake.

As most turkey hunters will readily tell you, in nature, the hen almost always goes to the gobbler. If those of you with feminine parts find this objectionable, all I can say is that it is nature's way. The guys strut around and gobble and the girls come running. In order to kill a turkey one has to make him go against his natural inclination. He has to come to you. You cannot achieve this by yelping – "I'm coming –I'm coming!" –every time he asks. Instead you have to convince him that you are the pin-up version of everything he ever dreamed about, and just a little too busy to have to walk over to all that gobbling noise. In other words, you shut up and let him do most of the talking.

One should never turkey hunt with a watch on, but I was doing it. I tried to rush things and staged a mock fly-down while it was still too early. He heard it. He got real excited, and real vocal, and really attached to his limb. He could see a good long way in any direction and rightly assumed that this chick would be visible any second. I never made another sound but because of that blunder he didn't leave his tree until seven forty-five. This operation had a hard deck of eight-fifteen.

Once he was on the ground it was time to re-establish contact. I yelped, clucked, cackled, purred, and cackled some more. He, of course, stayed in place and out of my visual range answering every noise that I made. On any normal day it was now time to give him the silent treatment and maybe get a look at him down my gun barrel in thirty minutes or so –but it was eight a.m., desperate measures were called for.

There is an area around a strutting turkey that I call his zone. It varies in size with individual turkeys and with the topography. Outside this zone he answers you, maybe, but won't come. Get inside this zone and you definitely have his attention. Sometimes it is almost within gunshot, and quite often unobtainable. If he sees you it is game over.

There was no topographical feature that was going to allow me to get any closer. My only hope was to move when he had his back to me –but I couldn't see him. The only option was to do it by ear.

When a turkey struts he has his tail feathers spread out which blocks his usually excellent rear-peripheral vision. When he gobbles while facing you, it sounds closer, louder. When he turns the other way it sounds farther. He may be strutting back and forth only a few steps, but it sounds like he is moving twenty yards in each direction.

I started the dreaded, almost-never-works, tree-to-tree creep. Slowly, silently it went, pausing frequently until I felt like he was, or might be, facing the other way. After about a hundred yards I felt like I should be in viewing range –by then I was ground-slithering only, ever so slowly. A large tree was just in front, only a few feet away. If I could make it there I would stop, ease my back up against it, gun ready, and make a call. I made it to the back of the tree and slowly eased my head net covered face around the great bowl at the base . . . there was a low gasp, a startled movement –my call fell out of my mouth . . . I was looking into the frightened eyes of a head net covered face belonging to a very young negro boy.

He could not have been more than eleven or twelve years old, was armed with a single shot twenty gauge, and wore a full suite of camouflage including gloves.

The turkey gobbled again, close.

This was not the time for relaxed conversation. In as silent a whisper as possible I asked, "Are you loaded?"

He nodded his head, still wide-eyed.

"Have you been calling?"

He shook his head –no.

"You got a call?"

Another head shake.

The turkey gobbled again, closer… very close.

"Put your gun up on your knee and get ready," I told him, and don't move!" –as I tried to slide silently back behind the tree.

It was a big tree, and I couldn't see the kid, or if he was ready, but it hid me fairly well. I lay flat on my belly and gave a few yelps, which were answered immediately, and followed this with a cackle and some leaf raking with my hand for realism. The gobbles got closer and closer until I was sure that the boy had frozen, or forgot to load his gun maybe, but finally the shot rang out and I peered around the tree to see him racing for the bird.

"That your first one?" –I asked.

"Yes suh."

"Did you call?"

"I don't have no call."

I was puzzled –"What made you decide to go turkey hunting?"

"Been watchin it on TV."

"Is this your first time?"

"No suh, I been heah ever mo'nin fo the las week waiting on this here gobbler, but he neva has come my way."

Wow, that boy had earned this turkey. "Anybody in your family hunt?"

"No, jes me. My daddy gave me the huntin videos."

By this time we were both walking back toward the road. I had heard no other car that morning, and this kid was a bit young to drive, so I asked him, "How did you get here?"

"My bike" was the answer and sure enough, a few yards further on we came to an old blue stingray, hidden in the woods.

"Mister, can you push my bike? I really want to carry my turkey."

"You bet."

He had ridden, or walked, the bicycle into the woods, somehow, in the dark and by himself. Not only that but he had been doing it every morning before school for a week!

When we made it out to the gravel road my truck was nearby. I loaded boy, bicycle, and turkey in the truck and drove him down the road to his parents' trailer. Along the way he received a half dozen of my homemade calls and a five-minute lesson on how to use them. My guess is that he mastered their use right away.

It has been quite a few years now, since that day, and I keep expecting to see some good looking young black man take over the turkey hunting video market, but it hasn't happened yet. Maybe life's road took a different turn for him than the one I saw him on. It would be a shame. One thing that I know for certain, those gobblers down Cedar Grove road were in for some mighty tough times!

Unsung Heroes

A s I may have mentioned, once or even twice, duck season is too short and too precious a time to waste any of it. Robert Sparks and I were roommates at Mississippi State University and, though we participated fully in what Starkville had to offer, or even a little too fully at times, we were really missing the great duck shooting that we had grown up with. Especially the mallard shooting along the Mississippi River.

Somehow, probably through Robert's dad, we had an acquaintance with a Mr. Edgar Hood out of Tunica, Mississippi. He owned a piece of the famous Beaver Dam Lake and extended us an open invitation to come over and hunt, anytime we wished. Beaver Dam is an old Mississippi River oxbow lake and was made famous by the writings of the late Nash Buckingham back in the glory days of fifty duck limits, fly rods, and mint juleps. Needless to say, we wasted little time before showing up at his house.

Edgar was a tall, lanky fellow with a big smile and a slow, very southern, drawl. A noted personality of the non-mainstream variety, people tended to either love him or hate him—we found him to be a kindred spirit.

It turned out that he was going to be too busy for any duck hunting (he had just received his third, I believe, mail-order bride) but he told us to "Head down to the lake and kill all the ducks you want to."

Those were the kind of instructions that we appreciated, and, as it was late in the day, we dropped the boat trailer in his yard and headed across muddy fields towards the lake. The plan was to split up and scout around both sides on foot in order to formulate a plan for the morrow's shoot, and, dropping Robert off on the east side, I then headed around to the west.

Thick canebrakes were prevalent on my side, which made visual observations of the water difficult or impossible. The lake was up fairly high due to a deluge of recent rains and all I could do was walk the field edge watching, listening, or occasionally taking the well-defined deer trails down to the water's edge.

I had gone no more than a quarter of a mile without detecting any ducks to report when the first step into one of the aforementioned trails, kicked up the trail-maker. The old 870 pump-gun leapt to my shoulder and the five-point buck went down with a charge of number four pellets in his neck. No follow-up shot was needed at that range and, this was my first-ever buck, and the only one that I ever took with birdshot.

It was dark by the time Robert and I met at the vehicle. Neither of us had seen enough ducks to write home about and we assumed that it was because the river, less than a mile away, was flooding and all the waterfowl were being pulled away by freshly flooded new – ground. Robert's trek had produced a turkey and a couple of the big fox squirrels and so some time was needed to process our game.

While these chores were being attended to the options for our duck shoot were discussed and it was decided to hit the river, early. We would put in at nearby Trotters Landing and try the newly flooded timber upstream before making the three-hour drive back to Starkville and regimented duties.

Daylight found me backing down a forty-five degree incline composed of loose riprap, logs, and some small portions of concrete. An earlier flashlight inspection had caused us to hook the winch cable to a large cottonwood tree and lower ourselves down with the cable. My Blazer was a stick shift and anyone who has ever launched at a similar site will understand the clenched posture of my posterior anatomy. Even with the cable secured one should keep the windows open and have an ejection plan in place—Robert gallantly volunteered to direct from outside the vehicle and man the trailer winch.

It was obvious from the condition of the ramp that the Corps of Engineers were not planning to use this, one of their many access points up and down the Mississippi, anytime in the next decade, and so we left the trailer in the water and the winch tethered to the tree.

As we motored slowly through the timber, Robert probing with a paddle to find shallow, and therefore "ducky" conditions, large flocks of turkeys kept rolling through the tree tops, alighting after only a short distance, and re-flushing again at our continued approach while squealing wood ducks barely skittered out of the way, diving under water, often as not, and flushing after we had passed by.

Soon, bunches of mallards circling above the treetops in the distance gave us a clue as to where a ridge could be found. As I slowly slid the boat through the trees in that direction, Robert kept up a constant report of the depth: "No bottom… no… just touching… getting shallower… you can wade here."

No shooting was done as we gently pushed the ducks out of their secluded spot, and, as we both preferred shooting while standing up, over the side we went into the waist deep water.

We didn't put out any decoys and they were not necessary. It was a cold clear day with a brisk north wind and ducks were migrating down the river en-mass. They were coming out of the sky from somewhere way up, wings locked, and looking hard. Our duck calls were limbered up and soon we had a rotational hurricane of mallards above. This was a day of take-turns type shooting, greenheads only, and it is amazing how much better one shoots in such a situation; taking your time, looking for a good opening, let 'em go around again if necessary—shoot when you are ready and hit or miss. We were young then, had good eyes, and I think we hit fairly often—or at least that's the way I remember it.

Our ridge was narrow, and only tiptoe, elbows-up type wading in most places; consequently some of our retrieval had to be put off until we could get back to the boat. After an hour or so, soaking wet from repeated dunkings, we called a halt.

I went and got the boat and then, with Robert on the bow for grabbing or cripple shooting, we finished up the retrieval process. It was not entirely a surprise to find that we had too many ducks… several too many; and now somehow a turkey had found its way into the boat… was it even turkey season?...—not sure.

We tied the excess cargo in a bunch and motored back to the launch site—scanning the trees and brush along the way for hidden danger. My nervousness existed on several levels: first, I didn't have any money; second, my dad would not be happy if I got a ticket—at all; third, I had already gotten one the year before, a dove hunting violation but federal nonetheless, and I didn't think two would be a great idea.

There was no one visible, hiding in the bushes, and no strange vehicles in sight. We had heard nothing, all morning.

Right then I had a bad feeling. I can't explain how, but it's true. Many times over the years I have been able to tell when I was being watched. Call it what you will, but something or somebody was there.

The bank was very steep and choked with brush except at the very top where it leveled out. If somebody was watching us they had to be up there and the only time when we would not be visible was coming up quick—right against the shore and just down from the ramp.

Trying to make it look natural, I eased the tiller over just a bit and headed for this presumed blind spot. Only a second or two pause, hardly noticeable, and we coasted up to the ramp.

We were stiff with cold and could barely move, a condition forgotten in the preceding few moments. The ramp was too steep a place to try to get out of our now full of water waders and so we loaded the boat on the trailer and winched ourselves to the top first.

The green truck just appeared in front of my bumper. I never saw where he came from and never heard him coming. One of the largest and toughest looking men that I had ever seen stepped out in full game-warden uniform. He looked over the situation, asked us a few questions, and saw that we were terrified and almost hypothermic.

"Ya'll get up on the tailgate and I'll pull off your boots."

We did as told while he, with the largest hands I have ever seen—hands as big as dinner plates, and powerful— gently helped us out of our waders.

"My name is Wilber Hanks," he volunteered, "and you boys ought to know better than to get out on that river in this kind of weather. No duck or deer is worth a man's life, and believe me, I've pulled out my share of corpses."

"Yes sir."

"Now ya'll git on outah he'a an be mo careful in the future... you hear?" While he talked he looked all around and back at us in a knowing way that sent shivers through our spines.

"Yes sir, thank you sir," was all that we could manage.

We drove away for an hour and then snuck back to get the stashed cargo, hoping, fervently, not to meet Mr. Hanks again.

———————

Seven years later, married, one on the way, I moved my budding family to a farm in the Delta. The nearest town was Lula, Mississippi. Most small towns in this country, and the world for that matter, have a meeting place where the men gather to talk and drink coffee. In Lula it was Harold O'Brient's parts store. The first person I saw upon entering this establishment for the first time, was Wilber Hanks.

Mr. Hanks had retired by that time and spent a good portion of his time at the coffee club telling tall tales. Most of the people in town had been caught by him, more than once, and joined in the telling of these tales. It was only then that I became aware of the reputation he earned, and the incredible effort that he had used, in the defense of our property, rights, and the fish and game of our state.

We became friends, of a sort, and Mr. Hanks hunted, occasionally, on my farm with my permission. He asked me if I would take him on a really good turkey hunt. The way he said it made me think that he was viewing this as a one-last-time type event. He said he didn't know how to call turkeys—never had to learn there were so many when he was a young man—and so I, of course, volunteered to do so.

It was a perfect morning in mid-April when I walked with the old gentleman, side by side down the dark logging road. Moving slowly, on his behalf, we managed to get in position well before gobbling time. It was one of those rare and treasured mornings when one gets it just right. By daylight we had ten turkeys gobbling at every sound I could make, all within two hundred yards. Five of the toms strutted our way, in full view for most of the way and gobbling at every step. I was situated ten yards behind Mr. Hanks and unarmed. He had his gun up, pointed right at a gobbler that looked to be about twenty-five yards away... the minutes ticked by. After a while the turkeys walked on off and Mr. Hanks put his gun down and smiled back at me.

"I just wanted to 'be there' one more time," he said.

Back at the truck I had to tell him the truth about that time out on the river. It had been bothering me and something told me that I had better not wait any longer. I told him the story, apologized for being a slob, and hoped he would forgive me.

"Son, ya'll didn't fool me for a minute. I was all set to bust the two of you, but when I got a look at you, all soaking wet and scared to death, I decided that you might have already learned your lesson. I let you go that time. And from what I hear tell, you've been perty good ever since."

I was shocked, but thankful... all this time. And, come to think of it, I'm certain that he played a part in my reformation. A really good game warden has to be judge and jury at times. Not many realize how big an effect that they can have on people's lives.

Wilber Hanks died a few months later, I believe, of cancer. He will be missed by all the people whose lives he has touched in his profession, and personally. I am one of them. If they give awards in heaven to game wardens, Mr. Hanks is at the top of the podium.

L-R Robert Sparks and author Starkeville, Ms.

Rios

Ted O'Brien, or "Black Top" as you shall soon learn.
Don't know the reason for all the camo.

The eastern half of the United States has a lot of turkeys and a lot of turkey hunters. Meleagris Galapovo Sylvestris, more commonly known as the Eastern wild turkey, is the species found here and it is a challenging bird to hunt. It is generally believed to have binocular vision eight times better than a man and hearing several times better also. Very little curiosity and an exceedingly distrustful nature round out the package. No Eastern wild turkey hunter that I know of expects to get a turkey every time he goes into the woods. In fact, most people that I know are happy to get one or two a year, and they are people that hunt a lot.

Part of the difficulty inherent in the pursuit of Easterns has to do with the terrain. Eastern turkeys live in the woods. It can be thick or thin, swamp or hills, or a combination of all, but generally the preferred habitat is mostly forested.

Picture yourself strolling through the woods. Last year's dead leaves are unavoidable as are the occasional dry twigs hidden beneath. Limbs must be bent back to allow passage at times and the occasional deadfall must be climbed over along with its surrounding mass of dead limbs. No matter how careful you are, even if your great grandfather was Geronimo, there is going to be some noise.

Now picture a flock of wild turkeys slowly feeding along in a distrustful manner. Half of them are standing dead still at any one time, heads up, and scanning for danger. Remember, they can see you many times further than you can see them – and they are looking. Hard. They can also hear you – way before you might be able to see or hear them, and they are ALWAYS listening. What are your chances of getting a glimpse of this flock?

This is the bird and the terrain that defines the term "turkey hunting" for anyone who lives in the eastern half of the country.

Other species exist in the western half and the most numerous is the Rio Grande subspecies – Meleagris Galapavo Intermedia. I assume that Rios have the same finely tuned senses as their eastern cousins, but they act completely different. This could be because of the terrain they inhabit. Rio are a bird of the arid, more open country. Typical good Rio habitat is open, scrubby, grassland with only occasional patches of trees. In some areas, due to the lack of decent roosting sites, Rios will even roost on the cross bars at the tops of wooden telephone poles.

Growing up in this open country they can see long distances. People, horses, cows, vehicles – all must be encountered regularly. Therein lies the crux of my theory: if just the sight of something dangerous sent them into a panic they would all starve to death, in hiding.

Another aspect of their behavioral difference that is related to habitat is range. They travel a lot. Sparse, prickly vegetation, scant rainfall, and poor soils make food harder to find. Thus, in a days' ramblings a Rio will cover many times the distance traveled by an eastern cousin.

Rios gobble a lot more frequently and at more periods of the day than do easterns. Within dense populations they can be counted on to begin gobbling well before daylight and continue, off and on, until after dark. This too might be attributable to terrain. They can see other turkeys, in the distance, most of the time; and because a mile or so is no big deal to a Rio, any girls around might be attracted to a fine sounding gobble!

Another noticeable difference between Rios and Easterns is that Rios will quite often roost in a particular grove of trees, sometimes in large numbers, and possibly even year-round. This gregarious affinity for a particular spot makes them easier to locate and hunt. Although large numbers of gobbling turkeys will quicken the pulse of any true turkey hunter, it does not necessarily make them easier to kill near the roost site. There is usually so much gobbling, and so much yelping, fighting, and activity, that the lone hunter yelping plaintively in the distance is easily ignored. After fly-down, and once the different bands have spread out and started to move, calling becomes effective again. The same scenario holds true for Easterns when they too, occasionally, band together in very large numbers.

My first introduction to the Rio Grande turkeys was in Texas. A group of mid-southerners including myself, Bert Robinson, Ted O'Brien and Robert Weaver booked a hunt at the fabled Mariposa Ranch near Falfurrias. Forty-five thousand acres located deep in the heart of South Texas, the place was said to be a paradise for game.

None of us had ever hunted rios before, except maybe Bert, but we had all heard the stories. People we knew to be only average turkey hunters would go to Texas and kill four turkeys in two days of hunting. People who had never even turkey hunted before would get fine old gobblers with ten inch beards and inch and a half spurs – on the first day. Some people claimed to have heard thirty gobblers gobbling, all at once, and from the same half-acre roost. These mythical sounding tales had been dismissed until, over time, they built up enough substance to achieve the veneer of truth.

And here we were, in this alien looking landscape devoid of anything that could decently be called forest and where no self-respecting turkey that we had ever met would call home.

After landing at the airport and securing a vehicle we proceeded down the long, straight, South Texas highway in the direction indicated by our map. Cactus and mesquite thickets lined the roadway obscuring our view, most of the time, with occasional open stretches where one could see vast expanses of tan-ish looking grass, which seemed to grow in clumps with sand in between. An occasional cow might be visible, forlornly standing in the blazing sun. Man it was hot!

Finding the gate to the ranch was a challenge, but eventually it was located by the method of "keep going further" and a fairly conspicuous sign, if one was in the right place to see it. Our directions then said to "proceed down the main road to the headquarters." About every mile or so down the crushed shell, or caliche, road there would be a fence and a gate. These gates were of a design unique to us and, after experimenting with different methods, it was discovered that one need not exit the vehicle to go through. These were bump gates. You drove up to them, bumped them with the correct force, and they slowly swung open and then back closed. Timing was critical as was the amount of force administered – luckily we had insurance on the minivan.

At about the second bump gate, as it clonked closed behind us, turkeys were heard gobbling at the noise. We rolled down the windows and sure enough, five big gobblers were strutting, oblivious to our presence and less than fifty yards away. We all stared out the windows in disbelief. Surely they were not wild?

Soon the sightings became more frequent as we went through gate after gate. We stopped and called out of the windows – they gobbled back! We hooted – they gobbled, we beat on the sides of the van, honked the horn, anything – they gobbled back! Several times we had to stop the van and let turkeys get out of the road – gobbling!

The subject was discussed that maybe this was a no hunting area, a preserve so to speak; or maybe it was an advertisement – something to sucker people in and then they were sent out to hunt the real wild turkeys. Like I said, none of us had ever seen anything like this before.

Upon our arrival at the ranch headquarters there were turkeys strutting in the mowed grass of the yard when we got out. An older cowboy/gentleman came out to greet us and, noticing our unwavering attention on the turkeys, asked if we had ever hunted rios before. Finding out that we had not, he proceeded to explain to us that "The turkeys hereabouts are gentler than the turkeys back East." Most of them were shot, if at all, with rifles during the deer season – as a bonus or when somebody wanted a fresh turkey dinner. The spring season had only just been established and the turkeys didn't know it yet. They had "never been called to before." None of the other ranches around there thought that anyone would pay to hunt turkeys but it was getting so popular in the east that he thought they might give it a try.

"And we have forty oil and gas wells here on the ranch. Every day, somebody has to drive up and check on every one. Along with our usual ranch activities, these birds are used to seeing vehicles."

I noticed a bit of drool starting to hang from the chins of several of my companions who stood with me in the dark, cool, ranch house interior. As our host continued our indoctrination I could see that everyone's attention was locked on the bright plate glass window, overlooking a small fountain near the front door. Leaning slightly over to gain a better view, I froze in place also. Fifteen yards from us a magnificent gobbler tilted his head back and let the cool water run down his wattles. I needed a handkerchief.

We had two mornings and two afternoons to hunt, and the ranch limit was two birds – unless one chose to pay extra. That first afternoon a Mexican vaquero dropped me off at a shooting house. This was just a plywood box built maybe six feet of the ground with a chair inside and a window to shoot out of. A corn feeder stood about twenty yards away. He bade me to get in and then took a bucket out of the back of the truck and began spreading corn on the ground all around my stand. This made me a little bit nervous. I realized that things might be done differently in Texas, but baiting was a crime back East. And baiting for turkeys was so socially unacceptable, so terrible, that one could be ostracized from decent company for life, kicked out of a hunting club – never invited back again, or excluded from personal inheritance of any kind. Yep, this was a bit different for sure.

I climbed up in the gun house and watched the ranch hand drive away – shaking the bucket with a few kernels left in it out the window as he drove. Turkeys started gobbling immediately and raced to the feeder. It was the first and only time in my life when I was actually trying to kill a turkey, and passed up a shot at a gobbler, or several in this case. A whole flock of turkeys, four or five toms included, greedily pecked up all the corn. I watched breathlessly through the crack at the bottom of the door as a trophy caliber Rio, beard dragging the ground, came under the ladder barely an arms length from my perch. A little while later they all began to drift away and I watched them go. It was not that I wouldn't shoot one of these same turkeys given another chance; it was just not going to be like that. I had to call one up, away from the feeder... but maybe not all that far.

I got out of the box and circled around in the direction that the big boys had taken. When it felt about right I kneeled down and gave a call – immediately several turkeys gobbled back but some distance away. Planting my back against a mesquite bush, gun ready, I called again. They answered right away and were already upon me. A big red head showed itself over a low rise and gave a resounding gobble – I pulled the trigger... and killed a jake. I did not know it at the time but another way that Easterns and Rios differ is that jake Rios gobble like men – a lot.

That evening four very excited hunters gave their individual stories in the age-old and customary fashion: in detail, without interruption, until they were finished. Questions followed, as they always do, and in such a way do turkey hunters compound their knowledge of the bird.

Bert was finished, two big beautiful toms. He said that he was calling... but not too loud. Robert had brought back a real monster with inch and a half spurs, his first ever, and was not ashamed that corn was still trickling out of the bird's mouth. Ted, the best caller in the group, had struck out. It was a rare opportunity to have one-up on Ted and we were merciless... in a nice way. He was also probably the best turkey hunter and prided himself on his ability, as most men do who excel. This, of course, made the day even better for the rest of us as we each, in turn, gave him our professional advice on how to deal with the Rios – what are friends for?

The next morning I asked the ranch hand not to put me out anywhere near a feeder. He obliged and dropped me off well before daylight on a sandy knoll where I could hear a great span of country. Turkeys were gobbling already in several directions and it was nowhere near daylight yet. After a long walk I ended up at a large roost with probably twenty or more turkeys gobbling – there was no way to get an accurate count. They did it in a wave, like in a stadium. A gobbler on one end would start off and the guy next to him would try to cut him off and so on down the line. It just flowed back and forth and was the most beautiful music that I had ever heard. When it was light enough I began to call and at the start of the first yelp of each series every turkey within hearing would gobble back. Gun up on my knee, finger poised over the trigger, dims shapes strutted and fought, well out of range in all directions. This went on for about an hour, and then, everything became silent. They were all gone… How could I have that many turkeys answering me and not even have one stumble by accidentally?

After another hour or so I decided to climb up in a giant live oak tree in order to get a better look around. The tree's limbs spread out wide from the trunk and paralleled the ground for a good ways, thick as a man's waist and sturdy. It was an easy tree to climb and made me envy those South Texas kids who had these to play in.

Up off the ground visibility was much better. I could see some turkeys in the distance and gauge their reactions to my call. Soft calling brought no response, but after a loud call they would gobble. I could see their heads throw forward, and their bodies shake, but no sound reached me. The big wide-open spaces seemed to swallow it all up, like a sponge.

Eventually, I spotted one coming in silently. He looked like an old tom, a loner. He was already inside my grove of trees and he was looking for me. His posture told me that he was wary, alerted. Under the canopy of the live oak grove nothing grew. Aside from the trunks of the actual trees, visibility was excellent – and he could see no hen. A couple of low clucks, muffled and uncertain, were all I dared but it turned him, just enough. He passed by at thirty yards and died in mid-stride. That turned out to be a very good thing because, for future reference, you can't get out of a tree very quickly to go and chase a wounded bird.

The truck came to pick me up a little while later and Ted was already in it with a nice pair of gobblers. I gave him all the details of my arboreal turkey hunt, but he was less than forthcoming with his own.

"Did they come in together?" I asked.

"Naw, they were nearby but not together." Hmmm…

"Did you have to move or just set up one time?"

"Yeah, I was moving… moved yeah."

Back at the camp and after much group detective work and deliberation it was determined that Ted had shot his turkeys out of the truck and off of a paved road just east of camp. Greed is listed as one of the seven deadly sins. God's punishment, in this case, was unique. After due and inspired deliberation, it was decided that henceforth and forevermore, Ted, would be known to one and all, by the nickname… "Black Top."

Robert did not get one that morning but Bert had taken another pair. I now know, after many similar trips, that Bert is a shooter. He is not one to pass up a good opportunity or waste much time about it either – he has the killer instinct, thinly veiled beneath an affable manner.

After lunch Robert wanted to borrow a slate call so that he could try to call up a turkey by himself. We went back behind the house and I demonstrated the loud way to call that can get answers from a great distance. Each time I called we both thought that maybe a turkey had gobbled in answer, during the series. It was hard to tell for sure but the fact that we both thought we had heard it gave some credence. Most yelping series consist of three or more yelps. I told Robert that I was going to yelp twice and he should move away a few yards and determine where this gobble was coming from. We tried it and I saw Robert turn and tiptoe quietly over to the corner of the house and slowly peer around. A couple of hens were pecking their way across the side yard with a gigantic gobbler strutting behind. Robert ran to get his gun while I stayed to keep track of the turkeys. While he was gone a Mexican came out of a small shed that was nearer to the turkeys. He had on a white T-shirt and carried a white bucket and just walked right by them and into a side door to the kitchen. At no time was he within shooting range of the birds and they did no more than just watch him go by. If the turkeys kept on in their current direction they were going to pass that shed pretty close.

When Robert returned I told him what I had seen. He quickly procured a T-shirt and bucket and stepped out from the corner, gun held low along his leg and somewhat out of sight. Whistling a tune and casually walking along he made no eye contact with the turkeys. Once he had gained the visual protection of the shed it took but a moment to go to the far side, ease the gun barrel around the corner, and wait for them to step into sight. I could see the turkeys and see Robert the entire time. I gave one more call and the turkey gobbled again – almost past the corner of the shed. A few seconds later Robert became the only person I have ever heard of who killed a turkey by camouflaging himself as a yard boy.

We went back to the Mariposa a few more times over the years, always with success, but the numbers of turkeys encountered were steadily going down. I don't know if this was a natural cycle or the product of commercial hunting, but it was obvious.

Other places were tried: the Big N in West Texas where the turkeys stayed out in open pasture all day only returning to the single creek where the trees were after dark; Fort Mckavit Ranch where one hunted within a high-fenced area full of bison, elk, and exotic goats; L'il Toledo Lodge in Kansas where one might see a Rio and an Eastern strutting side by side. All of these places were fun, and different, but did not have the sheer numbers that we had first experienced in South Texas.

John Stokes, his son Jack, myself, and their Uncle George were planning another foray after the Rios. We wanted to experience the real South Texas "best" and it was Bert who found it for us and let us in on the deal. It seems he had just come from a trip to the King Ranch and had experienced a hunt like the Mariposa used to be... only a lot better.

The King Ranch is vast and has many divisions. They hire top-notch wildlife biologists and managers, and give them management goals to achieve. The biologists set the "take" limits and then outfitters lease the block and operate under the given rules. Some areas are managed with the emphasis on trophy deer, some for quail, nilgai, or turkey. Up until that time one area had been reserved for family only. It was a pristine, low-yield place – a preserve so to speak. That area was called Tio Moya – the crown jewel of the King Ranch.

No account of our first visit to Tio Moya would be complete without a brief synopsis of the travel involved. It seemed straightforward: one flew to Dallas and then to Brownsville, rented a car, and drove to the ranch. Simple really.

John, Jack, and I had for various reasons booked only a two-day hunt. We were to arrive about two p.m., hunt that afternoon, the next day, and the following morning if needed. Our flight out of Brownsville was at two p.m. on the last day. A tight schedule to be sure.

We arrived in Dallas on time and went to our next gate for the last leg, which was only about forty-five minutes later. For some reason all the bags for the coming flights were being piled up on the floor and then transferred to another room. Flights were being delayed somewhere and people were getting bumped right and left. It was crowded, hot, and loud. Thunder rumbled and the sky became black. The time for our flight came and went. Confused and angry passengers crowded the Delta check-in desk and broke in front of what might have passed for a line. When our turn came we found ourselves standing before a very effeminate looking male gate attendant who told us that the flight had been delayed an hour – no problem. The new departure time came and went… we had been delayed another hour… more people showed up, displaced, angry people. It seems the flight was over-booked; would anyone please give their seats up now? If not, random selection would begin immediately, we were told.

It was getting late and Mr. John was getting livid. We, Jack and I, could tell something big was about to happen. "Boys, ya'll go get our bags. I'm going to rent a car. I think it is only about four or five hours driving time and we could have been there by now!"

Jack and I proceeded to the desk and told the very harried looking guy that three of us were going to give up our seats and drive, "could we have our bags please?"

"The bags are already checked." –was the reply.

Jack pointed out that he could see our bags over there and we could get them ourselves.

Nose held high, the man said, "I can't release any bags!"

We went back and told John about it. Exasperated, he said, "You boys don't know how to get things done – I'll show you!"

He marched up to the desk and demanded our bags, and was refused. "Hell I can see them right over there! And my pills are in there which I need right now!"

"What kind of pills?"

"Digitalis. I have a bad heart!" as John slumped over the counter and rubbed his chest, obviously in great pain and suffering.

"Call a cab. I will look up the address of the nearest pharmacy."

John's face turned an angry red, not sickly, angry, and his voice thundered over the background noise, "Listen you little punk, I know the president of this airline and if you want to keep your miserable job…" His finger was jabbing perilously close to the little man's chest and actually touched him, causing him to step back.

"Are you threatening me sir?" came in a high-pitched shriek.

"You dam right I am!" as the finger made a direct and intentional contact this time.

Jack and I were already backing up when the little man picked up the phone. Two doors at the back of the crowded room immediately slammed open and a couple of burly uniformed officers began pushing their way toward us. John spun around and whispered, "Scatter! We'll meet up at baggage claim in thirty minutes!"

Jack and I took off running. More security was coming down the long corridor from the other direction – they had us boxed! Some stairs led us to a lower set of corridors. We ran a long way and then took the stairs back up a level. A tram appeared, we took it – anywhere…

Thirty minutes later we met Mr. John at baggage claim. We had traveled miles to do it but he, on the other hand, used the crowd, and a newspaper extended in front of him at times, to slowly filter through the net. A master at camouflage, no wonder he was such a good turkey hunter.

Because we had to go to the airport in Brownsville anyway to pick up our gear, it was deemed prudent to leave this one, where our pictures were no doubt being circulated at this very moment, and go to the other one. There, in fresh, new, un-chased surroundings we could buy another ticket to Brownsville and hopefully retrieve our stuff without getting arrested.

John footed the bill and we actually beat our bags there.

We got in too late to hunt or see much of the country but it was apparent that this place was a lot more wooded than any we had hunted before. Huge live oak motts predominated, some covering hundreds of acres and with big mesquite flats interspersed throughout.

A tall, lantern-jawed young Texan by the name of Jim was our guide. Born and raised on the ranch he had a slow Texas drawl and a dry wit, which combined to make him an excellent companion. He was ready, well before daylight, waiting in an old Willis jeep. He didn't say a word as he drove us out in the dark and it looked as if we were traveling through an endless tunnel formed by the over-arching limbs of the giant live oak trees. For no apparent reason, and without a word of explanation, he stopped the open jeep in the middle of the road and just sat there. After a few awkward seconds where nobody moved or said a word, John asked "What . . ." and fifty turkeys at least gobbled at the same time – directly over our heads and on all sides. I looked up and was staring at the underside of a turkey – five feet away. Jim chuckled a little and without a word commenced driving. There was turkey shit all over the jeep and us: now I see why Texans wear those big hats.

We thought that it might be a prudent plan to put one of us out here. "Nope, we're go' in on down the road."

None of us had ever heard that many turkeys before and John decided to push the issue a little. "But we don't like to hunt together, we want to spread out."

"You'll be spread out."

Out of curiosity I asked, "How many roosts are on this place?"

"Bout forty." Was the matter of fact reply.

"Oh . . . – are any as big as that one?"

"Yep, some a lot bigger!"

"Oh . . . wow." That pretty well silenced any more of our questions.

Jim let us out at different roosts, far apart at Mr. John's urging, and told us to go in any direction we wanted, he'd find us whenever we were ready. This seemed a tall order on a thirty-three thousand acre ranch criss-crossed in all directions by roads, trails and trees, but there was nothing for it but to take him at his word.

My roost probably had from eighty to a hundred Toms gobbling in it. There is no possible way to get an accurate count in a situation like that, so one just has to guess. It was a live-oak grove that covered an area maybe a hundred yards wide and a half-mile long. Thirty minutes before daylight, when I first got there, they were already wave-gobbling. They might have been doing it all night. I stayed back away from the roost and just listened. At sunrise, they all started to fly down in several different locations. The strutting and the fighting started, not just between the gobblers, but all the turkeys, young, old, male and female. Most of it was for show – just reaffirming dominance and hierarchy – then the preening time came in preparation for the new day. Well back and out of range I didn't even call. The gobblers separated into groups, probably by age-class, consisting of ten or more birds per strutting group. Nearly motionless, they formed large, black, humps out on the sparse prairie grass openings and when clustered together looked like low, dark, hills, faintly flowing as they slowly leaned their fans from side to side. Thirty minutes later they began to move off, hens first, toms following. Another half hour and I began to hunt.

This was what I called "run-an-gun" hunting, as opposed to careful, slow trolling. Run-an-gun is accomplished by covering ground quickly, calling often. When a turkey answers one moves in close, very close, before starting a dialogue. The plan is to either kill him or scare him away, without using up a lot of time doing it. Invariably some turkeys are spooked by this method, but here, that was not a problem; there was always another gobbler, or more often group of gobblers, strutting away just a little farther on.

I spooked several while learning the terrain but when Jim somehow miraculously ghosted up in the old Willis I had an ancient, long-spurred trophy and could have shot several more. Jack was already in the jeep with his bird and couldn't believe the game he had seen in the last few minutes while riding around. Jim told us that John, the old sage, had killed early and was back at camp with a Bloody Mary. It was about ten-thirty and we asked Jim to show us around until lunch, which he was glad to do.

We rode through oak motts, mesquite flats, sand dunes and coastal plain; we saw deer by the hundreds; nilgai by the dozen – a huge species of antelope imported from India – and turkeys, gobblers mostly, in every type of habitat. Sometimes there were ten or more in a group, all strutting, and usually in a line of sorts. We saw HUNDREDS of gobblers! Many of which just gobbled at the jeep as we passed by. We experimented with which was the best shock-gobble technique – owl calls, coyote howls, crows, whistles – they all worked, the louder the better. It was a rare moment in life when, without speaking about it, we both knew this was paradise on earth.

Arriving back at the camp we were met by a most satisfied group of turkey hunters. Uncle George, a renowned agronomist, turkey hunter, and Mississippi Delta planter, had brought his two sons along and they were all through – sort of like the fox in the hen-house scenario. John, it turned out, had killed two, and was wrangling for another pair – the state limit being four birds but the ranch limit was set at two. A little while later, and somewhat poorer, he had the go ahead.

We spent the early part of the afternoon sitting in the shade of the porch overlooking a small, fenced-in courtyard overshadowed by giant live oaks, a water tank, and a corn feeder. Stories were told, of course, each and every bird was discussed, but the main attraction on this long, hot afternoon was the constant stream of turkeys coming to eat and drink in this shady oasis. The porch was situated so that a gate was at one end, left open for the animals, and from the porch's slightly elevated position one could watch the birds walk, or strut, into this protected place and feed mere feet away. It is difficult to describe the feeling of calling to a flock of wild turkeys— many of ancient age— from six feet away and in plain view, and having them gobble back with gusto. After a while a large boar appeared, sauntering in amongst the turkeys. We drew our legs back up, which, in some cases had been hanging off the porch, and commented on his savage appearance. After a few minutes, and taking no notice of us at all, he presented his other side to us. Printed clearly, in large white letters for all the world to see, were the words "DON'T SHOOT". To this day whenever discussions lead to the wonderful times spent at Tio Moya, the pig we called Don't Shoot is always mentioned.

By the second morning I was the only one left with a turkey to kill. Somebody had a video camera, a large, silver, boxy thing at that time, and we decided that we would all go together, all call together, and try to capture a fly-down from the big roost over the road.

My team lined up down both sides of the dry, white, caliche road and tried to get well hidden in the dark. I found a log pile, which gave an elevated visual position and great cover. On cue, the turkeys started gobbling and the team started calling. Cackles and fly-down noises came from all up and down the road and the toms went crazy. In fact, we jumped the gun a little and there were probably twenty toms strutting in the road before it was light enough to shoot. The drumming sounds seemed to come from all around, more a feeling than a sound, and the grating of forty or more stiff wing tips on the ancient sea shells made it sound like a giant earth mover was slowly coming down the road. The turkeys seemed to prefer this noise but the road itself would only fit five abreast – and so they just lined up in waves, like on parade; warrior chiefs going off to battle. I let the first few waves go by, not because I couldn't get a shot, but because I couldn't shoot without killing multiple turkeys. I almost didn't shoot at all . . . almost.

For many years following that fateful day we made an annual pilgrimage to Tio Moya. Over time the ever-increasing pressures to squeeze a few more dollars from the ranch for an ever-increasing number of King Ranch heirs depleted the turkey stocks somewhat. Even then it was still the best place on the planet. Eventually a very wealthy individual leased the whole thing . . . and we were out.

If you ever get to hunt Rios, and find yourself next to a really big, historic roost, on a good turkey year, my advice to you is to say a prayer to God, thanking him for the opportunity . . . and then just sit there and listen.

The author with an Eastern and a Rio, taken with one shot.

Li'l Toledo Lodge, Kansas

Mr. John, Jack and myself— Li'l Toledo

"Uncle" George Ray Walker— expert agronomist,
farmer and turkey hunter.
Those are some hooks!
—Tio Moya

Don't Shoot— Tio Moya

Self Defense... ?

When in the woods or out on the waters, things happen sometimes that are out of the norm. Most of the time we are happy to relate these experiences to others —either seeking corroboration of similar experiences or just to add to the general body of knowledge on the subject. Sometimes, maybe only once in a lifetime, and if you are lucky, something happens that is so far fetched, so bizarre, that you don't talk about it because you don't think that anyone would ever believe you. Naturally you would tell a kindred spirit, or maybe two, just to test the waters so to speak, but seeing the doubt on their faces you would then just decide to shut up about it.

I have been shut up for quite a few years now and it is high time that I get to tell my story. It happened just like I am about to relate and if you don't believe it, that is your business. Small-minded people can hopefully evolve, and in time, be coaxed into the light with the rest of us.

As far as I know, unless there are other silent victims out there, I am the only person on earth who has ever had a fight with a wild, wild turkey gobbler. I'm not talking about a crippled turkey, or a turkey in a pen, or a turkey caught in a fence or vines. I'm talking about a real wild turkey in the woods that could have left me alone if he had wanted to.

It was Easter Sunday, 1992 give or take a year, and a perfect morning for gobbling. Clear, cool, no wind, you could not have special ordered a more perfect day for Christ to rise from the dead or to be in the woods at sunrise. My good friend and neighbor, Allen Johnson, had invited me to hunt turkeys on his place before church. He is a Baptist, and even though they don't drink wine in church, some of them are still good people, and good hunters too. Anyway he had a lot of turkeys, was the only one hunting them at that time, and I readily accepted the invitation.

I met him in his driveway, in the black-greyishness that predates dawn by an hour at least, and asked him where we were going to go. He said, "Barn-Hill" as that was where most of the turkeys seemed to be. Allen is a farmer, a better one than I, and like all farmers everywhere we name places by certain geographical features or inherit the names and they just stay that way for generations. There was no barn at Barn-Hill –probably hadn't been since the mule-plowing days—and not much of a hill either, but that is beside the point, it has been, and always will be, Barn-Hill.

When we got out of the truck at the edge of the woods it was still fairly dark and turkeys were gobbling both left and right. Allen told me that the birds on our left were mine and we split up, girding our loins for battle.

Sound is a tricky thing, in the woods and early of a morning. My birds didn't sound very far off, but I immediately encountered water of unknown depth and extent. The woods are flat bottomland, mostly oak and hickory of the more water tolerant varieties, and at that time were beginning to leaf out. Sound carries exceedingly well over water but vegetation muffles sound to a great degree. Phillips Bayou meanders through these woods and was now in flood, as it is every spring, but there might be slight ridges out there that were dry, or at least semi-dry. Those turkeys could be planning to fly to my bank, the far bank on the other side, or a ridge in between.

I started wading in hopes of finding a ridge. After two hundred yards there was no land, but the turkeys didn't sound any closer. Another two hundred and it was the same situation. It was possible that I was being lured out into the water by a tag team gobbling effort where the near bird would gobble until a certain point was reached and then his cronies further on would take up the work, or, possibly, the sound was just finding a clear path to my ear from some great distance away.

A turkey's gobble is one of the most elusive, baffling, sounds in nature, second only to the sandhill crane. Sometimes it can be heard for miles and other times one can barely identify it up close. Being half deaf, in my case, doesn't help very much.

By the time I had waded half a mile it was getting on toward fly down time. A low ridge finally appeared, but it could not be approached without spooking the turkeys. While perched in the trees they had an exceptional view of the ridge and surroundings and I was quite sure, now, that the roost sight was directly over that ridge.

After a few minutes of waiting time a couple of turkeys' here-to-for unseen flew down ahead of me and over the next few minutes several more sets of wings could be heard. There was a large blow down, which is a tree that has been toppled by wind, between myself and the turkeys' assumed location and so I quickly waded to the shore with the intent of sitting beside the first suitable tree encountered. The plan changed dramatically when the tip-tops of the fans of five strutting gobblers became just visible over the downed tree and about to round its near end, about thirty yards away. I took the first bird in line without ever having sat down or making a single call.

A different rout was taken on the way back to the truck, a long loop, mostly on dry land, and eventually an old logging road was encountered which seemed to be headed in the right direction.

I'm a fan of roads, whenever possible, and have found that in most instances the roads are there for a reason and one should use them. Whoever built this road was trying to get logs and equipment out of the swamp, without getting mired up in the mud and therefore losing time and money. A good logging road will always follow the high ground and always lead you out –at least, that is, if you are following it in the right direction.

This one took a fairly straight course through recently un-flooded timber. It was probably several decades old and traversed an area of now very large timber with a dense over-story which, providing shade, kept the ground level free of undergrowth. Visibility was good and because of this I saw the white of a gobblers' head about two hundred yards away. He was walking down the road that I was on and coming my way.

My first reaction was to freeze, of course – one always freezes in these situations. He then went out of sight for a moment and I took this opportunity to plop down on the ground beside the nearest tree, which was a cypress. It had a big bole, flared at the base, and several large knees. Nestled against it I was cradled by the curvature of its form as if in a reclining chair at home.

He came into view again, but only for a moment as the distance closed. I put in a mouth call and hurried to get my head net and gloves on before he appeared again – I was going to try and have some fun.

The cypress tree was right on the side of the road and my legs were actually sticking out into it a little. The dead turkey was lying beside my right leg as was my gun and if I didn't move them they were going to be in the gobbler's path.

Occasional glimpses showed me that he was still on course, walking steadily my way and unaware. I needed to hide the dead bird and gun out of sight, but I was running out of time. At about the same time when one would put his gun up, when the turkeys vision was obscured for a moment but he was about to come in range, I grabbed the dead turkey and set it between my legs, facing away from me, and with a wing over each knee. It didn't look right that way and so I grabbed the loose skin on the back of its head, with my gloved hand, and held the head and neck erect. In this position I remained motionless and watched the big gobbler approach. Just like when you are hiding from a person, motionless but in plain sight, he did not see me, or the turkey held in front of me, until he was ten feet away. It scared him out of his claws –just like it does to a person.

This in itself would be a fine story to tell at a hunting camp, but we were just getting started. For many years I have practiced gobbling with a mouth call. It sounds okay, but rarely do I use it in the woods and when I do, the results are invariably inconclusive.

The turkey jumped strait up about five feet and landed with eyes as big as oranges. I gobbled and he cut me off. I started gobbling repeatedly –so did he. This was really getting to be a lot of fun and so I went into a fighting purr mixed with gobbles –and he attacked! My dead bird was standing up, wings spread, and must have looked threatening. Feathers flew and the impacts had the force of hammer blows. It happened so fast that it was difficult to see or react to, and he kept coming, time after time. After the first couple of hits I had my head turned away, to protect my face, and was just using the dead bird as a shield- no more gobbling or fighting purrs, or hiding for that matter. I was ready for this to be over but the enraged tom came in close, stood on my gun, and tried to push the dead turkey and me over with his chest.

At that time I decided that enough was enough and threw the dead bird at him. The attacker and I stood eye to eye now, and he was not scared. I put my hands out, to protect my eyes – he was still within striking distance – and shouted, "shoo bird!" in a very loud tone, and "Get away!" –he stayed. He had become so fighting-mad that his brain could not process what his eyes were seeing. With an ominous fighting purr building louder and faster he began pacing a half circle around me – not the dead turkey, me. Throwing off my head net but leaving an arm extended to guard against the next attack, I stood up. For a few moments he just looked at me like, "Who are you and don't get in my way," and then slowly, with apparent reluctance that it was over, he walked away – gobbling every now and then – the winner by a knockout.

I showed Allen the muddy footprints on my gun and the tear in the sleeve of my camo –the arm that had been holding the dead turkey's head. He had a camcorder and taped the story of the entire encounter . . . but I could tell. By a certain look in his eyes and a certain inflexion of voice, I could tell he really didn't believe it.

Three hours later church was letting out at St. George's Episcopal Church in Clarksdale, Mississippi. Our pastor, Ben Nelson, was also an avid turkey hunter. Along with my rarely worn Easter Sunday coat and tie, I had a brilliant, fresh turkey feather carefully displayed in my coat pocket –like a handkerchief. He, of course, noticed it and like any turkey hunter was curious for some details. I told him that yes, it was a beautiful day and made even more glorious by the fact that I had killed a turkey. That's all. The story of a lifetime and I was afraid to tell it.

Well, I guess the cat's out of the bag now –good luck, and you might want to wear goggles!

The Guide

The word "guide" is used to describe a person who takes other people hunting or fishing for money. It infers that this person has vast and mysterious knowledge of the habits and thought processes of the quarry in question. Guides always go to the right places and at the right times and always come back with a limit. How else could they be guides?

Wrong. Personal experience has taught me that there are more bad guides than good ones. A lot more. Like the time my dad hired a guide to take us duck hunting on the St, Francis; the guy didn't even have a blind and we got bumped out of every one he tried to put us in; or the Cree Indian I spent ten days hunting with in Alberta, Canada. I had tags for moose, elk, bear, wolf, and saw a lot of each – from a four-wheeler. His idea of the proper way to bow-hunt bear (you can substitute any other species for bear) was to drive the roads and trails until an animal was sighted, race up to the fleeing animal as close as possible, and yell "Shoot heem!" –from a moving four-wheeler.

Another time I hired a well-publicized snow goose hunting outfit in Stuttgart, Arkansas to take out me and a group of very special friends. Well aware of what it took in the way of labor and equipment to hunt the white swarms that cover the Mid-South every winter, I was very explicit with the outfitter before booking the trip. My group was not going to put out or pick up however many thousands of decoys that were needed –there were a good many aging and bad backs in the group and I wanted to hire a couple of young fellows to do it for us. This was to be a gift from me to my friends, a gentleman's hunt so to speak, and it was also the only way I could get my group to go. He agreed enthusiastically while giving me the highlights of the last few weeks of shooting. It seems the bad days averaged forty or fifty birds and the good days several hundred. There was no limit, "and bring a lot of shells!"

We arrived at the appointed time and place –a beat up house and barn on a muddy road in the middle of nowhere, surrounded by miles of flat, featureless, rice fields. The place was dark. No one was around. After a few frantic phone calls and an hour of waiting, a surly young teenager showed up along with the light of a new day. He proceeded to hook up a long flatbed trailer to a tractor and piled on lay-out blinds, and bag after bag of decoys, wind socks, rags, etc. He was alone. Next he ordered us all onto the open trailer and sped off into a thirty mile per hour headwind down the mud road. The dual wheels on the tractor picked up the gumbo mud, which wasn't quite frozen, and threw it back on top of us in huge, spinning, globs. Some of the largest of these were of sufficient size to kill or maim. The kid in the cab of the tractor didn't seem to notice, nor could he hear our cries of despair, which were muffled by the blinds and bags we had managed to slide beneath for protection. Just before the layer of mud reached the critical mass required for the squelching of human life, he stopped.

Sliding open a side window, just a crack, he yelled at us to get the blinds grassed up and put out the decoys. He, on the other hand, had to run back to camp, he had forgotten something.

There must have been a thousand windsocks, in dozens of bags, on the trailer. We piled them on the turn-row, along with the eight layout blinds that would be needed. Close inspection revealed that none of the layout blinds had a stitch of camouflage on them. As the guide drove away we took stock of our situation.

The field where we were to hunt was a vast, flat, cut soybean field. Basically bare mud. It had from one to three inches of water covering most of it. There was no material nearby to grass the blinds with, nor the three to four hours required to do it in. The blinds were not waterproof. There were no geese in sight . . .

When the kid came back an hour later we were all sitting on the bags, right where he had left us. I don't think he got a big tip.

We've all had the fishing guide who sits in the front of the boat and catches all the fish; or the famous and highly publicized waterfowl guides with the huge blinds that pack in lots of paying customers, but no ducks. The list could go on and on and I'm sure that you could add to it, but I think the point has been made.

On the other hand a good guide can really make the trip—and lots of fish or game taken is not the only measure of success. An agreeable disposition and honest effort are required to get into this category. Some biological knowledge is also important, not only of the quarry but also of the surrounding ecosystem, its history, and other inhabitants.

A good guide that you like, and is fun to go with, is a rare and treasured gem.

Most of us work at jobs that are not always fun nor always satisfying. We dream of sunny afternoons catching fish and duck call lanyards filled with bands. At daydreaming, I would classify myself as world-class. I have always been good at it and anybody who knows me will confirm that I spend a lot of time practicing. As a youngster I just knew that I would be a great guide. I pictured myself as the rustic outdoorsman in the picture with my grateful client, kneeling behind some Boone and Crockett ungulate. I would be the weathered sage on the polling platform, patiently pointing out piscatorial trophies to my willing and biddable clients. I would be the revered duck guide, booked years in advance, who always comes back with a limit – lanyards filled with duck bands and drake curly-tail feathers encircling my head like a crown.

In order to make anything happen in this world, something has to be done; something beyond daydreaming. It was this revelation that prompted me to answer the ad –"Wanted: young, active, individuals who wish to be fly-fishing guides in Alaska. Room and board, tips, no experience necessary."

When I contacted the guy, he told me that he needed two guides, and did I know of anyone else who might be interested. I certainly did, Clayton George, a good friend with whom I was at that time sharing a very dirty summer job cleaning out burned barges on the Mississippi River. Clayton was an avid outdoorsman and a good man in wild country. I was sure he would jump at the chance, and so we set up an interview and got the jobs. It had begun. I was now on the first rung of the ladder leading towards fame and fortune.

Our employer, David, was an ex-trucker who had homesteaded a spot on the Talachulitna River, about one hundred and fifty air miles out of Anchorage, Alaska. After a ten-day drive from Hot Springs, Arkansas, where our new boss spent his winters, and with "Claybob" and I alternately riding in the back of the truck, and a brief float plane ride to top it off, we were glad to be there. The views were magnificent, the river full of salmon, and the accommodations agreeable.

We spent the first few weeks hauling gear up the hill and beating back aggressive vegetation with swing blades. In the land of the midnight sun, things grow in the summer. They grow like crazy. For just a few short months every living thing packs in a full year's worth of activity in preparation for the long, dark, snow covered winter. In May, when we arrived, the days were already long and getting longer. No matter what the work schedule there was always plenty of daylight left for us to fish on any given day. This we took advantage of and learned how to catch king salmon, grayling, and rainbow trout.

Eventually the clients began to show up. They came by floatplane, as everything did, and were generally agreeable and competent fishermen. As the seasons changed so did the target species in the river. At first we caught kings, then the silvers showed up; next came the red salmon and chum, and finally ending with a small run of the pinks.

As salmon migrate up the river to spawn it is called a run. Runs tend to overlap quite a bit and vary in individual quantity and duration. At times we would have three different species in the river at once and each required a different technique or presentation to be successful. Claybob and I became adept at identifying each species rapidly, before they could pass by on their upward journey, and using the proper techniques to catch them. Many of our clients were better fly-fishermen than we were and mastered the skills we showed them.

We wanted our clients to have a great experience. Not just for the tips, but because of our newly acquired professional standards. Our employer, on the other hand, was running a business. He instructed us to carry each group, day after day, upriver in the jet boats to the same deep hole, on the same bend in the river, fish ten hours and return. Granted gasoline was flown in by airplane and the shear-pins for the motors were all used up the first week, but we found that chopped up nails would substitute for shear-pins, and that clients liked a change of scenery, as did we.

Whenever we could, we gave our clients what they asked for. Though strict confidentiality was assured, invariably the word got out. Our relationship with the employer became progressively worse. The term cabin fever originated in Alaska, in just such a place. By the end of the summer the river became too low for the floatplane to land. There were no supplies, no clients, just us . . . together . . . alone.

It happened late one night. The boss had been drinking, a lot, for a while. Things were said that couldn't be taken back.

I'm sure financial pressures were at work, in his defense, but that was not really my problem.

I got mad. The kind of mad that makes your ears ring and every cell in your body tingle. The kind of mad where you are looking out of your eyes but separate from your body, disconnected, thinking a mile a minute. It came to me that if I stayed there any longer somebody was going to get hurt, and, with the people involved, it was going to be serious.

Claybob was reading in the bunkroom when I came in. He sat up, looking at my face, and already knew what had happened. I told him I was sorry, but I had to go – now.

"I'm ready, don't know why we're still here," was all he said.

Here was the situation: We had just quit and were basically fleeing from what we considered a mad-man; we were over a hundred miles from a town and the surrounding country was snow capped mountain peaks interspersed with bog-land in between. There was another lodge a few miles upriver that had an airplane; sometimes they were there, other times not. Our former employer was not on speaking terms with them and so we had never met. With limited options, we decided to go there.

Each of us carried all of our worldly possessions: duffel bag, shotgun –loaded with buckshot for bears, tackle box and rod case. The riverbanks were covered in a dense stand of alders and impassible on foot. We walked in the river, upstream – the whole way.

The owner was there, and contrary to what we had been told, seemed a really nice guy. Unfortunately his plane was broken down, as was his radio. He said that there was a trapper's cabin about fifteen miles below and he thought the guy might even be home and have a radio. There was also a deep stretch of river just below the cabin where a floatplane would be able to land. He took us most of the way in his boat but had to let us out at the head of some rapids with only another mile or so to go.

When we walked out of the icy river, wet to our arm-pits and with all our gear balanced on shoulders and heads, the trapper stood watching from up on the hill. This wasn't exactly hikers' country and I'm sure he had never had anyone walk up for a visit. A large pistol was in his waist band and he invited us up for coffee. After a few cups and some time for us to dry out, he admitted that at first, he didn't know what we were up to. We looked ghost white, and a little bit crazy, coming up out of the river like that. He also explained to us that by Alaska state law our employer had to provide transportation for us when we were ready to terminate our employment. An unusual law designed to address a situation such as we were in –apparently not so uncommon in the wilderness of the far north. His radio worked and he made the arrangements for us.

Four hours and several pots of coffee later, the floatplane arrived and all was well, or so we thought.

The pilot, a rugged and capable man with whom we were already acquainted, informed us that he could only take us one at a time due to the condition of the "runway." It was a narrow, boulder-strewn section of river that ended in an abrupt, ninety-degree turn facing the steep side of a mountain several thousand feet high.

I went first, and, as the plane zigzagged between boulders trying to gain speed, I noticed how quickly we were approaching the sharp turn. A discrete glance at the pilot led me to believe that he was noticing it also. He was alternately trying to break one pontoon loose from the water and then the other, trying to get a bit of a bounce it seemed, and all to no avail. At the last possible second he reached up to his shoulder harness and cinched it as tight as possible, and then yanked back on the wheel. We cleared the last boulder by a foot or two and the alders on the bank by a yard. A few really nifty tight spirals within the canyon gained us enough altitude to clear the mountain ahead. On the other side, a world away and heretofore unknown to me, was a vast mountain lake. Miles across and a cold, shimmering blue, here was an endless runway for a floatplane.

He put us down gently on the mirror-smooth water and taxied to a large rounded rock, about a half-mile from shore, where I was deposited along with my gear. I then watched my transportation disappear back over the mountain.

At first I was just thankful that we had not crashed on take-off –thankful for the big lake and the nice rock, thankful to be alive. It was quiet . . . really quiet. The plane could not be heard at all once it passed over the ridge. After a while clouds rolled in, it turned cold, and started to rain. A few angry seagulls began to dispute my right to be on this rock. More showed up and they became aggressive. I squatted, on the lowest spot that could be found, with my face between my knees and arms folded over my head in a protective stance. Hours later, or so it seemed, the roar of an engine overcame the cacophony of birds as the plane cleared the far blue mountain. I was saved.

Author with a king salmon from the Talachulitna River

Clayton George with a fine silver.

Supplies coming!

It was many years later before I tried guiding again. This time I was going to be in charge.

Hog hunting was fairly new to the mid-south and I had a good pack of dogs and an excellent population of near pure strain Russian wild boar.

I advertised the hunt as no-kill no-pay and soon had a taker. The guy's name was Mark, I believe, and he had never been hog hunting before. As it turned out, I don't think he had ever been any kind of hunting before. No matter, we could handle that easy enough. In hog hunting with dogs, neither marksmanship nor stealth plays a big part.

I conscripted a couple of good friends, Charley Lowrance and Chris Marley, to aid in the endeavor. Both were avid and competent outdoorsmen and at the time, big into hog hunting and hog dogs.

We met Mark at my gate to the hunting lands behind the Mississippi River levee, which is where we planned to let the dogs go. I had determined that he was not a horse person and therefore had a pair of four wheelers ready— while Charley and Chris rode horseback to better keep up with the dogs. The wind was blowing hard out of the north and the dogs soon struck scent, and then jumped a hog that went straight south and out of hearing. This was in the days before GPS collars –we kept up with our dogs by ear. We split up in order to cover more ground. The dogs were probably bayed-up, somewhere, and we needed to get there fast.

As Mark and I rode south, along the western side of the levee, I inquired about his choice of weapon. It looked like a military style rifle, post and circle iron sights, vintage WWII probably. He didn't know what caliber it was, which seemed odd. I asked him if it was accurate. He replied that he had never shot it before . . .?

Within a half a mile or so, I could just hear the dogs, and they were definitely bayed. It sounded like a heck of a fight going on and we needed to get there quickly, or maybe lose some dogs. Over logs, through brush and weaving amongst the trees, we arrived as fast as possible and found the horsemen already there.

One of the biggest barrs (A barr is a boar that has been castrated at some point in the past) that I have ever seen stood backed-up into a buck-brush thicket in the middle of a semi-dried up barrow pit. (Barrow pits were formed when the corps of engineers "borrowed" dirt to build the levee. Now days they usually hold water for part of the year and are therefore devoid of tree growth.) Anyway, he had brush protecting his rear with open ground all around him, and he was mad. Most of the dogs were keeping their distance, many already with cuts showing that they had gotten too close. I told Mark to put a bullet in his ear from where we were, about thirty yards away, and do it quick. This barr looked like he remembered getting that way, and wasn't going to let it happen again. He weighed about four hundred pounds and had half-curl tusks, unbroken, which is rare, and obviously knew how to use them. Mark replied that he had lost his gun. A quick conference was called and it was determined that we didn't have time to find it. Chris produced a pistol and handed it to Mark who just stood there, unsure what to do. The big hog tossed another dog, which backed up, limping.

Charley was getting worried about the dogs and asked, "You want me to shoot him for you?"

"Sure." Came the reply.

Charley was riding by when he said it and held out his hand to Chris –"Hurry!"

Chris took the pistol and threw it across the intervening distance where Charley caught it with his right hand, on the right side of his horse, brought it around to the left side as the horse took two more steps, all in one fluid motion, and drilled the hog right in the ear – while moving. We thought we were looking at Rooster Cogburn!

The client paid me the money and took his trophy home, and we took six dogs to the vet and gave him the money. Somebody wins in every situation.

I decided that maybe dangerous game was not the best place to guide the average person.

The author with a wild boar in Mississippi.

Years went by without the itch to guide causing me so much as a single rash. And then the riverboat casinos came to town.

Edward Pidgeon and I had a large floating duck blind in Moon Lake. We hunted just about every day of the season and had pretty consistent luck that year. It was the first year that casinos came to Coahoma County, after they had been in Tunica for a year or so. They, the local casino named Lady Luck, had heard about our success and asked us to take out an occasional high-roller for them. Money was no object to them, at least it seemed that way, and we soon made a deal – perhaps we would meet some new and interesting people.

Our first set of clients met us at the dock and at the appointed time. Nicely dressed, polite, middle aged, they were obviously well to do folks. It was foggy that morning –so foggy that we weren't going to be able to shoot any ducks until it lifted somewhat, so we took our time getting out to the blind. The decoys were already out, manicured the day before, and the blind was well brushed and stocked with charcoal and anything else that might be needed. We had permanent jerk-strings rigged up to the surrounding trees and all running to a pulley, anchored to the bottom just in front of the blind, with a single rope going into the blind. By pulling that one rope, dozens of decoys were set in motion and ripples appeared throughout the whole spread. It was a fantastic set-up and no batteries were needed. The boat hide was completely enclosed and ergonomically designed. One just drove in, stepped out, and you were already hunting.

Going slow and careful, we finally ghosted up to the blind in the fog. When I tried to ease into the boat hide, I ran into something . . . another boat. This was a first for us here, at Moon Lake. We called out to whoever it was and said sorry, we were here now, as politely as possible. I then backed the boat out and waited . . .nobody moved. This was getting awkward. I then pulled around to the front of the blind and saw five unsmiling faces looking down at me.

"Hey guys," I tried to remain cheerful, "You are in our blind, we are hunting here today." Nobody moved.

In a slightly more forceful tone, "Gentlemen, we need for ya'll to go somewhere else if you don't mind."

A voice from inside the blind said, "we're not go'in anywhere."

"Hey ya'll, this isn't right, and we have some people with us from out of town . . ."

Some profanity started pouring out of the blind and I noticed our clients were wishing they were somewhere else – I couldn't blame them. About then Edward started to climb over the front of the blind and so I put the boat in reverse and backed him out of reach, Edward's negotiating skills are notoriously blunt.

To avoid what looked like it might turn into a battle, possibly with guns, I left those guys in our blind –that day. Other days would come, I was sure, but I wouldn't have clients then. And by the way, that was three strikes for my guiding carrier –I was done.

Los Remolinos

There is the old saying that the grass is always greener on the other side of the fence. What it means is that we as human beings are hard-wired at birth to want what we don't have. As an example that hits close to home, my wife wants a swimming pool, a jet airplane and a new body –not necessarily in that order. Before we get too deeply into feminine desires let me say that hunters and fishermen are not immune to this genetic phenomenon.

Every outdoors-person that I know of is constantly scheming to go off upon some supposedly greener pasture and shoot a different colored bird or catch a strange looking fish. For many, success can be measured by the number of different kinds of mounts that can be displayed, or maybe the size of the individual mounts in relation to the average for the species. As with precious gems, rarity sets the value. This, apparently, is a universal malady, there is no cure, and though the objectives of obsession may differ, no one is immune.

I am lucky enough to spend a portion of each annual cycle in North Dakota and the Mississippi Delta –both prime hunting locations. Consequently, I have friends and neighbors in both areas that love to hunt. The ones in North Dakota dream of shooting deer, just about any deer with a decent set of antlers, because they are scarce –the winters kill so many that the population stays relatively small. In Mississippi, where the winters are mild, we have almost no winterkill. Deer populations are a constant problem and a hazard to automobiles and crops as well as their woodland ecosystems.

My neighbors in Mississippi deer hunt almost every day of a very long season, while dreaming of a trip to the Dakotas in pursuit of the wily ringneck –which spends most of its yearly cycle cracking the windshields and busting the grills of North Dakotans. It is a fact that many more ringnecks are killed by cars than guns and that might be true of deer in Mississippi also.

It would appear that grass is only greener if you don't have to cut it; but occasionally, it really is.

It was a dull, rainy afternoon in February, in which I sat at my desk and tried to think up a suitable article for Delta Farm Press's next publication. My topics were all nature related, as you might have guessed, and because of all the grey and rain going on outside I was musing on funguses, morels specifically, when the phone rang.

Mr. John's rough, scratchy voice sounded through the earpiece, "Buck, Anne and I are going to be at Los Remolinos in March and April and we want you to come down there with

Jack and do some stag hunting. I'll meet ya'll at Cordoba and scholarship both of you on a dove shoot, including your shells, and then we'll all go down to the estancia and get our stags. If there's time –I just bought an inflatable raft for down there— we'll float the Alumine'; there's some great fishing on that river –maybe best in the world, and nobody floats it… ever!"

Well, it was going to be hard to focus on an article about mushrooms for a while.

John and Anne Stokes were co-owners, along with Henri and Marsha Wedell, of a large estancia, or cattle ranch, in southern Argentina. The place was named Los Remolinos which loosely translates into—"the whirlwind." Fifty thousand or so hectares tucked away back in the rolling hills of the arid Pampas, the place is home to many exotic, to me, species of game. Red stag (cierbo), emus, guanaco (kind of like a lama), perdiz (a partridge species similar to the California quail), and trucha (trout) were just a few of the species regularly seen or taken.

Interestingly, on a side note, though the country had its own wealth of indigenous species, the red stag, partridge, and trout were all imports from Europe. Apparently, many of the anti-Nazi Europeans fled Hitler's persecution to places like Argentina, and brought their favorite pastimes with them. They also brought along their genes, customs, and quite a bit of European ingenuity, which melded into a very unique and vibrant culture.

All of this was very green grass to me and it is needless to say that I jumped at the opportunity.

Our leaving day was to be the twenty-fifth of March and there was a lot to do. Passports and gun documents were needed and trigger fingers had to be exercised at the sporting clays range; fishing gear had to be fussed over and rifles sighted in for long range. Patagonia is big open country. The kind of place where you might wait all day crouching in the shade of a small, scraggly, thorn bush for that stag to give you a three hundred yard shot. Jack and I were definitely going to have to become "one" with our rifles.

I settled on a bullet weight of 180 grains for my 7mm magnum, tried a couple of brands, and then bought twenty boxes of the same batch number –an important detail, I learned, when one goes long range. Using the telephone poles, which were about ninety yards apart on the gravel road that runs through my farm, as distance markers, I practiced lobbing bullets at way past my usual two hundred yard range. Getting comfortable with a big holdover in the scope took a good bit of ammo and I made a point of shooting in tricky winds –a lot. I had a good bit of learning to do. It was the first time that I, a bow and shotgun guy, had ever really tried with a rifle and the same could be said for Jack.

The day finally came for our departure and, check lists complete, we boarded a flight in Memphis for Miami, there to spend the night in the airport in order to catch the long flight in the wee hours of the following morning.

Travel is always a stressful ordeal and my stress level was soon augmented by the fact that I had left my passport in Mississippi. The aforementioned long layover came into play as my invaluable spouse packed up the two young children, drove the hour and a half to Memphis International, handed the passport to a Delta representative, who in turn put it on the next flight to Miami, where it was hand delivered to me in the nick of time. What a way to start a trip!

Passports in hand, guns and baggage already checked, we then boarded Areolinas Argentinas big seven-fifty-seven wide-body for Buenos Aries non-stop.

As a fan of the great historical fiction writer, Patrick O'Brien— who wrote so prolifically and in such detail about the lives and living conditions aboard the wooden sailing vessels in the eighteenth century English navy— I must say that the interior of this vessel and its numerical accompaniment, were copied right out of one of his stories. The coach section, where I was, literally seethed with humanity of all types and varying degrees of personal hygiene. The airline had also placed what appeared to be porta-poties, five of them in a row and of the common chemical-filled variety used at construction sites, in the center of the plane, and within about eight hours they were all full. The aroma was compounded over time for our enjoyment, as I am fairly certain that no fresh air was ever introduced. The smell would be something like what the old "slaver" ships were said to be like –below decks of course. I would recommend anyone making the journey to bump up to business class, if it can be afforded... or take a boat.

Arrival in Buenos Aries is followed by a customs check. Americans with guns are taken deep down into the bowels of the airport, away from all lights and noise from above. They are left in small, dimly lit rooms, there to sweat for an hour or so while seedy-looking officials argue loudly in a foreign language nearby. Eventually a small, even seedier looking man shows up and demands a hundred dollars. If you are lucky you may get to leave right then, but it may take a few more twenties if anyone else is standing nearby. It is amazing to me that almost everyone you meet on the street in Buenos Aries can speak several languages, and most certainly English, except the officials working in the customs department at the airport . . . interesting.

Our next flight was only a couple of hours south into the province of Cordoba –a well known destination for high volume dove shooting. Our guides met us at the airport and transported us in vans through a countryside of small towns and row-crops; the only noticeable difference between this and rural USA was the occasional roadblock with an officer standing there with his hand out… more twenties.

Lodgings were secured at a beautiful old Spanish mission called Santa Maria. Tile floors, wood burning fireplaces –kept alight in every room–gravity-flow toilets ingeniously operated from a roof-mounted tank, all added to the exotic feel of the place; not to mention the parrots, hundreds of them, who fed in the unique monkey-puzzle trees in the yard. All in all, the place was a welcome balm to the weary traveler.

John and Anne, along with Henri and Marsha, had by then joined forces and the excellent Argentine wines accompanied our open-fire assada and subsequent planning for the next day's shoot.

The Stokes and Wedells, being old hands at this game, had brought twenty-eight gauge guns and planned to shoot only one case of shells in the morning and one in the afternoon –apiece. This was considered the gentlemanly, sportsmanlike way to do things. Jack and I, however, had been listening to stories of crack shooters taking three thousand birds in a day using multiple guns and loaders. We decided to get it out of our systems, once and for all. Our goal was going to be "un mil," or a thousand apiece, with only one gun and no loader. We didn't realize it, but this was a tall order to fill.

The next morning found us scattered out on a brushy hillside apparently somewhere between a dove roost and the agricultural fields that they were heading towards. Unlike the dove shooting in the United States, there was no feed of any kind at our location and the doves all came from the same direction. They came in flocks of from ten to fifty at a time and usually less than a minute apart. The flight never slowed down the entire morning until right about noon. Over the course of no more than five or ten minutes, the flocks all lit in trees wherever they happened to be, and not a bird was to be seen in the air – an excellent time for lunch.

Jack was shooting a twelve gauge Kriegoff and I a magnum Remington 3200 –both heavy guns without much recoil. We compared notes at the campfire and we both had shot around seven hundred birds apiece. It seemed do-able, if they started flying again, but we were both somewhat worn down just by the lifting and loading of the big guns, and furthermore, blisters and worn places were beginning to show up on our anatomies. Band-aids were necessarily applied to the places where they would do some good and we were ready to go again.

About two o'clock the flight started back up; like as if someone had flipped a switch. All the trees and brush around us had doves sitting in them and they all just started moving again, over the course of only a minute or so, and in the direction from whence they had come that morning.

Jack was the first to reach "un mil" and was glad to quit. I finished up my last hundred pretty quick by just going for the easy ones. When my bird boy shouted "un mil," I didn't even shoot the shells that were already in my gun. With a deep breath, I slowly took the shells out and the earmuffs off, and just stood there, watching, in the orange glow of an already setting sun. The flights grew larger, closer together, going faster and faster, on and on, until individual flocks could no longer be distinguished— and as the light faded there was only a solid grey mass, maybe a quarter of a mile wide, seemingly endless, in either direction.

We shot doves for a couple of more days, but held ourselves to the case in the morning and one in the afternoon scenario. It is a lot more enjoyable that way, and if I ever go back that is how I will do it. Killing just for numbers sake leaves a bad taste in one's mouth, and for anyone who has a problem with limits, like Jack and I used to, Cordoba can cure you. It will also cure anyone of offering to buy your shells –Jack and I alone shot twenty-nine cases during the trip!

I am often asked what we did with all the birds. It is a valid question, and one that almost any person, sportsman or not, would ask. I thought that I had the answer—the party-line answer that most outfitters give when asked – and while shooting on my first day, I mentally congratulated myself, a pat on the back so to speak, for helping to feed so many needy families nearby. During a short pause in the shooting I even managed to ask my bird boy, in a mixture of hand signals and "espangless," what he was going to do with them. His answer, though not wasteful, was somewhat deflating: he fed them to "los puercos," his pigs. No matter where you go, value is directly proportional to scarcity.

A very worn-out Jack Stokes with "un mil!"

Our party was eager to try for the stags, and so the Southern Cross beckoned us onward. We arrived in Patagonia via San Martin De Los Andes, a small and picturesque gaucho/ski slope village, here to pick up a few items of local clothing etc. before embarking on the four-hour drive to Los Remolinos. I rode in the baggage truck along with a young gaucho named Egiardo. He spoke a little English, I a very little Spanish, and somehow we managed to communicate. He patiently answered my many questions about the flora and fauna that we were passing by, and proved a bright and very engaging companion. Even so, I am sure he was elated when he made the turn onto the homemade suspension bridge which heralded our arrival onto the lands belonging to Los Remolinos.

The house itself was picturesque, and unique in my experience. Perched on a gentle slope and with a trout stream down below, tall cliffs rose up behind upon which the red stag stayed during daylight hours. Every few minutes one or more of the noble beasts would give forth their own peculiar call— which can only be described as a roar— the sound being a close kin to the roar of an African lion. It is a haunting, melodious sound, not difficult to imitate, and like nothing I had ever heard before— far different from the bugle of a bull elk.

Necessity is the mother of invention and these same cliffs are the source of the water supply for the estancia, in the form of a high-up artesian spring, as well as its electricity.

The water is channeled into a pipe, which leads down the mountain, eventually under great pressure, and is forced through a turbine, which runs the generator– quite ingenious, and without fossil fuels, noise, or pollution of any kind. Leftover water is channeled to the house or the garden, and finally to the grass in the yard. This last use creates a green oasis in an otherwise arid region and draws the red deer in every night.

This last fact was brought to my attention the very first night when I was awakened by some clicking-clacking type noises on the window glass about six inches from my head. A closer inspection, maybe six inches closer, revealed a large red stag destroying the carefully tended shrubbery outside my window. The clacking noises had actually been his antler tips inadvertently tapping on the glass. Another one showed up and the ensuing roaring match kept me riveted to the window for at least an hour. The following morning I relayed the events to Miguel, the estancia's manager. With an exasperated sigh, he turned and looked scathingly at a large, ferocious looking dog. This worthy canine was employed full-time to drive the deer from the yard, he explained, but the dog seemed to disappear after sundown each day. It is my conjecture that he will no doubt live to pass on his fearless genes to future generations of guardians.

Day two in Patagonia the men-folk of our party were to engage in the pursuit of the great stags. The goal, as set forth by our hosts, was not just to kill a stag, but an "old" one. The emphasis is not so much on cubic inches of antler like it is here in the U.S., but rather on herd management. Old, worn-out, broken antlers, taken from an animal far past its breeding prime, are the most prized of all trophies.

My guide was Egiardo. Small and wiry, somewhere in his early twenties, he had been born on the estancia and had lived his whole life there—a good portion of it on horseback–and knew every nook and cranny of the entire fifty thousand or so hectares. Riding single file, he took me through lava and boulder fields, up and down canyons slick with loose shale and through thorny bush that could swallow a gringo forever. Not only was he a magnificent horseman but he also possessed the true instincts of a hunter. He saw every track, knew what the animal was up to, and, if necessary, altered our line of travel in order to see and not be seen. He saw everything except one important thing– a thing so alien to his way of life that it could never occur to his mind. He did not see that his "sport" was a horse-o-phobe.

I have been around horses a lot. I think that I am a logical, intuitive person, capable of making decent assumptions based on careful observation and evaluation of facts. An animal that has immense strength, coupled with little or no intelligence and a proclivity to start bucking, biting, kicking, or running, for no apparent reason and with absolutely no warning, is not my idea of the perfect hunting vehicle.

Every time I get on one of these beasts it starts tripping over its own feet, or pretending to. If I cross a swamp on horseback, in a line with ten other riders in front of me, my horse falls flat over on its side and wallows around for a while. I get the buckers that have never bucked before—"Wow, he's never done that before. Just keep riding up this narrow ledge a ways, he'll calm back down."; or the rollers who try to mash you into the ground—"He's a good horse but keep your feet loose in the stirrups, you might have to kick free!"; the biters/ kickers—"Don't never get close to his head or his hooves… but he's got a real nice stride!" This could go on and on but suffice it to say that I end up leading my horse home most of the time.

Egiardo and I looked at stags. The big herd bulls were spread out in the month of April tending their embras, which is the term for the female, and we had to cover a lot of ground. He led me through winding valleys and roundabout routes, never sky-lining ourselves, and crawled up countless thorn-covered hilltops to glass the hidden valleys where underground springs emerged. Each time I would see these massive antlers waiving in the distance, sometimes four or five sets in the herd, and I would ask "Viejo?"

"No, no viejo."

Not believing that anyone could tell how old a stag was from so great a distance I would invariably ask, "Quantos anos?"

The invariable answer would come "ocho", or "siete", and it would come with the calm assurance that a gringo horse-o-phobe could not question.

One evening as we made our way back to the little stone cabin in the hills that served as our hunting camp, my phobia was once again vindicated. It was just after sundown and, as chance would have it, our trail coincided with that of Jack and John's parties as we were crossing an open plain about a half-mile from camp. We were tired, almost home, and on flat and level terrain. No one was paying any attention to the horses as we just plodded along, telling stories of the day's events and in sight of the cabin. As usual, I was last in line when it happened.

Egiardo was in the lead and his horse came unglued, bucking wildly, and would not cross a shallow drain, about one foot wide and three inches deep. This started a chain reaction until every horse in the bunch was wild-eyed, snorting, and bucking –several pairs of reins were broken and one man was dragged a bit. Egiardo said it was a lion. Apparently a lion or two had walked down that shallow drain in the not so distant past. We were in the middle of a pancake-flat plain with sparse grass no taller than maybe three inches, visibility was absolute for a great distance in any direction, but there might as well have been an invisible wall between us and our destination.

True gauchos encounter this type of thing regularly, and they did get all our animals across eventually, but we gringos just walked on back and stayed out of the way.

The cabin at last, firelight, "soupa," and a warm sleeping bag– It is amazing how fast Argentine red wine can sooth one of riding sores, both mental and physical.

Dawn was breaking over towards South Africa when Egiardo effortlessly dismounted and looped his reigns over a thorny piece of brush. I did likewise, but with more effort, and stiffly followed him up the hill and to a rocky outcrop from whence we had a magnificent view overlooking the immense canyon formed by the Alumine' River.

Almost immediately roaring could be heard all up and down this vast watercourse. Probably fifteen hundred feet to the bottom and three quarters of a mile across, the river had carved this steep sided valley for miles and miles through the dessert. Occasional hints of green, other than that which appeared right on the river banks, could be seen near the bottom and seemed to indicate seep-water coming out from beneath the canyon walls—which explained the high density of deer down there.

We glassed a dozen or so herds from our perch; some were across the river, unreachable for us, but many were on our side. Big stags herded their embras into tightly bunched groups and frantically fought off all others who dared to come too near—lone stags marched between groups roaring a constant challenge along the way— only to be met by gleaming antlers, savagely wielded. We were ringside for what looked like the main event.

I had found a comfortable spot to glass from, one with a nice backrest and just the right seat, and was enjoying what looked to be shaping up as an equestrian-free morning, when Egiardo said, "Viejo!"

I followed his gaze to the bottom of the valley, near the river and maybe a mile upstream. There were definitely some dots down there, and with the eight-power Steiners, maybe some antlers.

After so many negatives I thought it probable that I had miss-heard. "Viejo?" I asked, pointing a finger.

"Si!"

".... okaaaay..."

We studied the herd and terrain for a while. Sometimes the ground looks a lot different from a different perspective and we were ideally positioned for the birds-eye view. It looked like, if one were down there next to the river that is, that there might be enough cover to get within shooting range. The problem was that we weren't down there. Most of the canyon had vertical walls, at least for part of the way, and then a good bit of slope that was so steep that no horse or vehicle could make it. Try as I might, I could see no way down for us.

"Vamanos!"

Well, I guessed he knew of a trail somewhere on down the canyon; alas, back to the horses we go —I had taken several steps in that direction before realizing that Egiardo had gone over the rim. I made my way back and cautiously peered over the edge. He had scrambled down a heretofore-unseen crack and was now strolling down a shale-covered slope with apparent ease.

Now, I am and always have been fascinated by physics. I was fairly certain that, with the aid of gravity, I could get down there, one way or another –but I was also certain that this self same gravity was not going to help me get back up. The decent was so steep, and so far, that I took it for granted that Egiardo knew some way to get the horses down there if we were lucky enough to shoot a stag. Thus, with the simple faith the ignorant so often possess, I scrambled down to catch up.

The bottom of the canyon was much flatter than it had appeared from above. Cattle and game trails crisscrossed each other and wound among the scattered brush and boulders while the roar of fast moving water drowned out all other sounds. Using hand signals, Egiardo led the way upriver with a steady breeze in our faces. After a half hour of careful stalking visual contact was made with our quarry. The herd had moved up the slope and was now grazing along the base of the canyon wall at a range of about four hundred yards and far above us. Their position was such that any further advance would result in immediately being spotted.

We crouched in the shade of a scraggly bush while the flies buzzed and the river roared behind us. I was hoping that the herd would feed our way, which seemed inevitable with the rock wall behind them, but it was not to be. The old boy was having trouble with some of his girls. Maybe they were getting tired of being pushed around, or maybe somebody had detected our presence, but several embras began to scramble up an unseen cleft, unhurried, but definitely leaving.

"Tiro!" said Egiardo.

I didn't like the shot. It was steep and far, maybe three hundred and fifty yards. I took a risk and scrambled forward about thirty yards to a pair of rocks that gave a solid rest with elbows and body braced.

"Tiro!" insisted Egiardo, "Tresciento meters."

Looked further than three hundred to me… but with the steep uphill shot a three hundred yard holdover would be just about right…

The old stag had waited for all twenty or so of his harem to disappear through a narrow gap and was just a step or so from vanishing also. Taking up slack on the trigger and giving the bullet's trajectory a little bit of a curve for the crossing wind, I tried to think the bullet home as the gun went off.

"Muerto!"

He said dead? After the recoil I couldn't see the stag nor any sign of one.

With feet, legs, arms, and head still buzzing with adrenaline I scrambled behind Egiardo up the slope. After crossing, and searching, several deep washes in the vicinity we eventually found our stag—dead in his tracks.

He was a true "Viejo" and we traded congratulations as we caught our breath. While Egiardo went to work on the trophy, I climbed a nearby rocky outcrop to see if I could spot the road… there was no road, just miles and miles of steep-walled canyon.

Scrambling back down, I asked Egiardo, "Donde es el camino?"

"No road" he said. At the same time he was finishing up trimming most of the meat off of the head in, what looked like, an effort to lighten the load.

"No caballos?" I asked. For the first time in my life I was wishing for a horse!

"Camiando… wee walk" says he.

With that he shouldered the eighty-pound head and started back the way we had come. Leaving all that meat was against my nature and so I quickly cut out a backstrap and hurried to catch up.

The climb out was a real struggle. I thought about abandoning my ten pounds of meat. At times I almost decided to leave my rifle, but it was too handy as a staff on the steep up hill going. What really got me out was Egiardo: this young man, about five feet tall and lean as a buggy-whip, was carrying an eighty pound load, and a sharp pointed and pretty darn awkward load at that. I was six foot five and maybe 190 lbs—I should be the one to carry the big load but I couldn't even catch up to make the suggestion... not that I was all that anxious to do so. We made it out, finally, and back to camp with fresh meat and trophy proudly displayed and in time for dinner.

Argentines eat beef, sheep, or goat, and do an excellent job with each of them. They do not seem to eat game, and when, at my insistence, the backstrap was served that evening everyone choked some down, politely, and gave what I have come to know as the universal signal of displeasure. We've all heard it, and used it, this signal, many times. It is a polite way to say "no I don't want to eat this ever again" or "this is no good at all –you really botched it up." It is a phrase that is used when someone burns the biscuits on the bottom or otherwise spoils the only item left to eat in camp. In turn, around the table, everyone agreed... "Its not that bad."

Mine was the last stag needed by the group and we returned to the headquarters of the estancia in triumph and took a day of rest while a great feast, or asada, was prepared. Stories were told over and over and the wine flowed freely while the cabrica hung on the crossed sticks and dripped fat on a low, smoky fire; colorfully sashed men with broad brimmed black hats, vests, and great knives tucked into their wide sashes tended the fires constantly, only taking occasional breaks for mate'— drunk from a gourd through a small, silver straw with a strainer on one end. For me it was a time of reflection;

a needed restful period in which the newly made memories could soak in and solidify. So much had I experienced, all brand new and exotic—the arid landscape, new and unusual animals and plant species, the people, culture… and it was all becoming comfortable.

Such a successful trip could easily have ended there, but we had the time, and John and Anne wanted to try out their new boat. An inflatable, it could easily hold a fisher-person at each end and a rower in the middle. There were four of us going and so John put Jack and I at each end with Anne sort of in-between. He took the rowing position because, as he put it, he didn't think any of the rest of us could be trusted to handle the craft properly.

We loaded rafts, gear, and people into two vehicles and made the three hour bumpy ride across the estancia to a put-in place along the Alumine' River. The plan was to float and fish, keeping a few for dinner, and stop overnight at another stone cabin that should be at about the halfway point. The worthy Egiardo was to meet us somewhere downriver, at a place he knew of but we had never seen, whenever we got there. Truly trustworthy employees are the rarest and most valuable of assets, and by now, we regarded Egiardo as family.

The Alumine' is a good sized river, as far as trout rivers go; maybe seventy-five yards wide on average with lots of deep runs and plenty of current. Spawned by glacier melt and augmented by underground springs, the crystal clear waters help drain the Andes as they travel a distance of one hundred and five miles through the arid Pampas, eventually to join the Collon Cura' on their way to the sea.

It is a beautiful river—majestic, and wild; basically un-visited or altered by the hand of man. It is also, and most importantly to our endeavor, chock full of trucha!

We started catching fish immediately, almost on every cast. Jack and I, with the tight quarters of the boat in mind, had brought light spinning rods and a small supply of Mepps and Rooster-tail spinners. The big rainbows and browns pounced on them like they had never seen one before, and likely they hadn't. Anne, a fly fishing purist, one also gifted with skill and luck, was keeping up with us, as she always seems to be able to do.

John was keeping count and even with pinched-down barbs we had boated and released seventy something fish, mostly in the pound and a half to three pound class, when Jack lost his last spinner. At a loss over what to do next he began digging around in the small tackle box that we shared and noticed the bottom shelf was full of bass style crankbaits– an oversight, of course. While packing he had simply forgotten to take them out –or possibly he was not worried about the space because spinners and flies don't use up much room in a box. Curiously, he picked out a three-inch crankbait in a crawfish color with a medium-deep running lip on it. His first cast was across a deep pool. He just had time to engage the bail before the rod bent double—resulting in a five-pound rainbow. The next cast netted an eight-pound brown and I was digging in the bottom of that box before he got the fish back to the boat.

We quit counting at one hundred and twenty-nine fish, many of the last fifty or so in the five to eight pound category with a few even larger. The little spinning reels with light lines couldn't fish the crankbaits in the usual manner and so they were just thrown out and mostly dragged across current until something hit, which was generally right away.

That night at the cabin we smoked trout as big as red salmon over the campfire and watched the Southern Cross and myriads of other stars that lit the sky up so brightly it seemed that daylight was just over the horizon. After dinner and with the fire burned down low, we lay on our backs and used binoculars to discover unknown galaxies and the age-old question, "are we alone?" was debated—as it has been by mankind through the ages—with the same answer always, "who knows?"

Day two was more of the same, but far less fervent in the fishing department—everyone was pretty well worn out. The scenery was spectacular, and we never saw another soul on the entire river—nor sign of anyone—even along the banks or as far inland as one could see.

About mid-afternoon we rounded a bend and there stood Egiardo, a welcome sight. We had a large stringer of jumbo trout for the estancia and, as everything was being loaded, I noticed Egiardo quietly hide the fish and cut our bass plugs off the lines. This, in itself, was logical enough but it was the way he did it that caught my attention. He was surreptitious, glancing around, and especially down the only road in sight.

"Egiardo, esta bien?" I asked.

"Si...bien."

I pointed at the hidden fish and the lure-free rods—"Porque?"

By then Miss Anne was listening and between us we began to understand the nature of Egiardo's uncharacteristic nervousness. It seems that the Alumine', or at least that part of it is a—1) Catch and release only; 2) Fly fishing only; 3) Barbless single-hooks only—type of a river. Like maybe a national park of some sort...

Jack and I just looked at each other, and then we both looked at his dad. No matter where we went, or how hard we tried, some things never change.

John W. Stokes Jr. with the intrepid Egiardo—
and a fine red stag.
Los Remolinos

Egiardo after the big climb— with author's stag

Anne Stokes— one of the great all-time lady anglers...
Maybe the greatest!
The Alumine' River, province of Neuquen, Argentina

John Stokes with a nice brown from the Alumine'

Henri and Marsha Wedell— at home on the range
Los Remolinos, Argentina

The Family Jewels

Many people take their sons hunting but not their daughters. I find this to be a basic crime against humanity, an affront to the feminine species, and even a darn poor way to do things.

The possession of a couple of "X" chromosomes, or the lack of a "Y" – however you want to look at it – does not make a person unable to appreciate some of the finer things in life. There are women painters, women sculptors, women businessmen – men apparently created the English language – and there are even women politicians. This last is very important because the politicians are the ones who are in charge of our game laws. They decide when we can shoot, what we can shoot, and how we get to go about it.

Even just an average pair of "X" chromosomes can vote, and they do it too. If for no other reason than this it should be apparent that it is in everyone's best interest to have a little knowledge and education spread throughout the gene pool.

As a dad the real reason one should take his daughter into the woods and waters is to show them something really special. Something you love and, though you may not talk about it, care about deeply and want them to also. Furthermore, a basic knowledge of something makes it a lot more interesting: one can join in a conversation; know when they are being kidded or made fun of; even make smart day-to-day choices that affect our environment and everything in it.

The actions of every person on this planet, every day, have some effect on every other creature on it. Think about it.

I happen to care the most about fish and game animals – the kinds that we hunt or catch. But that doesn't mean that I am against some lady who wants to save the dragonflies or nurture some exotic poison ivy plant in her garden. It's all interrelated really – without the dragonflies mosquitoes could suck us dry; without the poison ivy... well, I don't know what possible good there is in poison ivy, but I am sure there is something. My guess is that you get the picture without any more verbosity from me.

My daughters are grown now but I have fond memories of their outdoor exploits when they were of a much younger age. Neither of them became what one would call an avid outdoors person – probably my fault for keeping them in the boat too long because the crappie were biting; or in the duck blind too long because we just had a couple more to get – but they both understand nature, and hunting, and by golly they eat meat... at least some of the time, and aren't upset that something had to die so they could get it.

Sometimes our outings were pleasantly successful, usually because of advance work or preparation on my part. But in the woods, dealing with wild creatures, there are never any guaranties and they should know this. It is one of the rules that make the occasional successes that much sweeter.

Our first major outings were shed hunts – as in whitetail deer antler sheds. At this latitude in north Mississippi deer begin to shed the last year's antlers at the end of January and the whole population will get it done over about three weeks. A very few will keep their headgear much longer, sometimes well into the spring, but the vast majority have done it by the middle of February. It is my theory that the ones who don't shed with the rest of the population are either injured or have genetics inherited from another population indigenous to a different latitude. As you probably know, deer were moved around all over this country by various fish and game departments at one time. Who's to say that these individuals might not be expressing some of those genes?

February in northern Mississippi can be wet and cold, but in between these fast moving cold fronts there can be delightful weather. An afternoon's walk in the woods with no leaves on the trees so it is bright and sunny, no briars – they have all been devoured by deer at that time of the year – no mosquitoes, no poison-ivy, flies, ticks, or anything else to bother one is a pleasant outing. It is the perfect time to introduce kids to the outdoors.

Kids being gregarious creatures, we always had a big group of friends along with us. Having been a daddy for all of my little girl's lives, I had some insight into their psyche. It was my observation that they liked to win, or catch something, or find something – and pretty darn quick too. As far as I could tell this was universal for the species and an important piece of knowledge for anyone in my position.

I made it a habit to gather up as many sheds as possible throughout the year and keep them in a hidden spot. Just before one of these planned shed-finding outings, I would go out and "salt" the entire planned route. Everyone found some, everyone was happy, and they were recyclable for the next outing! Sometimes the girls would take them home, which was fine, but most ended up left in the truck and forgotten, along with socks, boots, wool caps and anything else that wasn't actually growing on them at the time.

Another fond memory was building and brushing duck blinds. We did not have suitable trees for the perfect tree house in our yard and therefore I substituted duck blind maintenance instead – at least until they got old enough to realize that I was getting some work out of them. I don't believe the real tree house families get more than a few years interest in that project either.

I can remember babysitting one weekend when the girls were about five and six, respectively. We were into the beginning stages of cabin fever and the yard was too muddy to play in. I suggested a boat ride and was immediately proven wise and omnipotent. We lived on a lake, still do, and it was a simple matter of getting in the boat and going. Nothing is really that simple with kids. It was cold, and so proper attire had to be found, then life jackets, Barbies – we probably had snacks even though the whole operation was not predicted to take over an hour.

My ulterior motive was to work on the duck decoys in front of a large floating blind that I keep on the lake. Water level fluctuations, wind, and two legged varmints team up to tangle the lines quite often and besides, it was time to pick them up for the year.

At any rate, we had a brisk and wonderful ride to the blind. The sky was blue, the water calm, and it was a good day to be outside.

My boat has a bass fishing seat on the front deck, quite a common occurrence around here, and once we got to the blind and quit riding the girls jumped into this seat. It sits on a pedestal and spins around easily. They were playing at getting dizzy. You know how you used to spin in a swing by twisting the ropes up as tight as you dared and then letting them untwist as you sped up or slowed down by retracting or extending your legs? They were doing that, sort of, up front. I was busy leaning over the bow and concentrating on a tangle.

I wasn't positive how I got there, but it was head first and very little splash – an Olympic ten I'm sure. Both girls were peering over the side when I came up. Both looked just like cherubs on a Christmas card – fortified by God against all evil and incapable of its contemplation.

"Why are you in the water daddy?" was said, and meant, with perfect sincerity... I think.

They've done their share of dove hunting, first as retrievers and then as shooters. My youngest doesn't like the kick or the noise of a shotgun and feels sorry for a wounded bird. If you put a 45-caliber pistol in the hands of this same delicate creature, with earmuffs of course, she will blast a can to bits exhibiting a predatory gleam all the while. The oldest likes to go, and shoot, but is far too busy to practice often enough to gain the proficiency she exhibits in all other endeavors with such ease. It is a fun social pastime, to be utilized on occasion and not worried about the rest of the year. She really is a fair shot, a natural competitor I guess, and could be great if she were so inclined – but is not.

Both girls have accompanied me on numerous deer hunts, especially when they were little – think babysitting here again – and most of the time I was very careful not to shoot a deer. I remembered the reaction to a wounded dove or duck all too well and unless the great stag of the forest appeared, I wasn't about to pull the trigger. It is interesting to note here that every deer we ever saw, and there were hundreds, was immediately accompanied by a tiny voice, in hushed tones, saying, "Shoot him Daddy!"

There is an interesting psychological anomaly going on there: Even with Bambi and The Littlest Mermaid showing anthropomorphic qualities – in my house on a daily basis – success was still the overpowering emotion. They wanted to get one.

My oldest daughter has shot a few turkeys and deer. She doesn't call turkeys, has no desire to learn, she just wants me to do it – which is fine. Days afield with one's daughter are rare jewels and become rarer, and therefore more valuable, as time passes.

My youngest doesn't wish to shoot deer or turkeys, or anything else for that matter, except cans, once she got old enough to say no. She's a good cook and enjoys eating game and is the luckiest fisher-person on earth.

She was home from college – a rare event – and was unusually receptive to my suggestion of a father-daughter outing. Perhaps she even missed me – gone for months at a time – which would be the only thing learned at college that I am particularly thankful for.

At any rate we were going fishing. Bass fishing. It didn't matter in the least to her that I had secured an invitation to Art Weimeyer's "Fox Den" fishing lake – chock full of giant Florida strain bass ready to jump in the boat if need be – she was just going to spend an afternoon with her dad.

It did matter to me. This place was unreal and I wanted to make sure she got a taste of it. Who wouldn't catch the fishing bug by reeling in five-pound largemouths until their arms were tired?

The night before, I worked on the boat and tackle. Everything was to be perfect. Word had it that the fish were hitting "slug-o's" – a kind of short stubby plastic worm that has the characteristic of sinking slowly without any weight. They are made of a fairly firm plastic and to be fished weedlessly one has to bury the barb of the hook inside of them – just like on a normal plastic worm fished with a slip weight. This just means that hook set is critical to get the barb through the bait and into the fish, and it takes a rod with some backbone to do it.

I rigged her up a salt water spinning outfit with new line and a swivel, to minimize the ever-present line twist that would show up after a number of fish were caught.

The afternoon was bright, blue, and windy as hell. Lilly-pads covered the lake interspersed with patches of open water and the wind kept trying to put us into the lilies, which fouled up the trolling motor. I gave her instructions on how to use the equipment and demonstrated a cast. After closing the bale and quickly handing her the rod I had to dash back to the trolling motor and try to head us into the wind. When I looked back she was stretched out sunbathing with an I-pod, sunglasses and a magazine open. Her rod was almost out of the boat – caught just by the handle on the lip of the gunnel – and line was peeling off the reel. She seemed startled that I was screaming at her. She did assess the situation correctly and calmly put the magazine down, picked up the rod, and keeping the tip pointed almost directly at the fish, began to crank it in. It weighed eight pounds. She then cast the bait a very short distance from the boat, laid the rod down, adjusted her I-pod and magazine and stretched back out. This time I caught the rod as it bounced my way going out the front of the boat. Yelling instructions, I handed her the rod and she cranked in another – it weighed seven. Then this young lady, the spearer of lobsters, killer of cans and participant in a once in a lifetime piscatorial event – never to be recreated or, in my opinion, surpassed – this young lady calmly reeled in her line, adjusted her music, and laid back down on the rear deck of the boat.

Like the deer who lose their horns at the wrong time – some genes just vary in a population.

These rare jewels of memory can be found in odd places and in unexpected circumstances.

My oldest likes to go duck hunting when it doesn't interfere with Mississippi State football or somebody's wedding. Both of these are schedulable events, it seems to me, and it is my opinion that if Mississippi State, or the couple in question, wanted me to come to the event they darn sure wouldn't schedule it during duck season.

She does like to go though, and I take great pleasure in the event.

Our club in Arkansas, "Blackfish Bayou", has a one-guest rule. So if I get to take her it is a one-on-one guided expedition. This is the only time when I remotely agree with or like this rule.

We received last pick in the draw for blinds that morning, after getting up at three a.m. and driving for an hour and a half. Normally I would spend the night at the club, having glassed the property before sundown for duck movements, and then get up at the civilized hour of five – but her schedule did not permit and that was that. The wind was out of the southwest and, with no scouting, I just picked a blind that would be favorable for the condition.

It was legal shooting time when we arrived at the blind and she helped me put out the decoys. We only had a couple of dozen, the water was shallow, and we just dumped the bags in the boat and pulled it along with us throwing as we went.

The early wake-up and hurry-hurry had thrown my schedule off kilter. Nobody under the age of forty would know what I mean, but when you get to a certain age things happen at a certain time – or your whole day gets messed up. Maybe it was the exercise, or excitement, but anyway my time had come – NOW!

I told her to get in the blind, load up, and shoot anything that came in – I had important business to attend to. This was not an easy proposition because I had on a lot of clothes, and neopreme waders, and we were in a boat. The only course of action possible was to get to land and as soon as possible.

It took me a while to get back to the blind. I was hurrying because my eldest daughter doesn't blow a duck call and wasn't going to have any luck while I was gone.

The blind is a tricky one to get in and out of. In my case it was better to just crawl off the front of the boat on hands and knees rather than trying to play Tarzan. As my head poked into the blind the first thing I saw was my lab, Rose, and a big pile of ducks beside her. Tail wagging, she seemed very pleased and not just at my return. I counted quickly, checking species – a perfect limit… for two!

"Hold up there honey, we're done!"

"Oh, I'm sorry Daddy, you didn't get to shoot!"

I couldn't have been any happier.

This is Claire, the eldest of the family jewels, with a nice turkey. She's the one who shot my ducks!

Dixie, the luckiest fisher-person on earth— but this time
helping out on a duck hunt.

The Perfect
Boat

Looking out over the harbor on Man-O-War Cay, Abaco, I can see many different types of vessels. Some are big and shiny with lots of bells and whistles. Others are equally large, but built strong, to carry stuff and do it in rough seas and high winds. These boats are generally scratched up and rugged looking. To me they depict the true nature of the relationship between man and the sea. I guess you could say they have character, like the men who use them.

There are many other types. Sail boats by the score –most of these are owned by winter people, snow birds if you will, who come here to escape the rigors of winter in the United States and Europe; they are almost all built more with comfort in mind than sailing qualities; they are floating homes, so to speak, able to sail, on occasion, but primarily used as a mobile home. They are generally shiny-finished fiberglass with catchy sounding names painted on the stern, along with a port of origin. I'm pretty sure not all of those boats sailed here from where they say they are from, judging from the people who are on them, or the painted names –Omaha? – but who knows. It would be impolite to ask.

Older sailboats are occasionally seen – after all, Man-O-War and nearby Hope Town, have been the boat-building hub of the Abacos for more than a century. In fact, outboard motors didn't arrive in Abaco – according to Steve Dodge in his wonderful historical work entitled "Abaco" –until the 1950's. These boats are usually wooden and shallow draft, made for the sponging trade of years gone by or the catching and hauling of various other commodities such as conch, whelks, and crawfish –which is what the Bahamians call the spiny lobster. These boats are fast becoming rare because wood doesn't last long in the ocean. Salt water and the denizens that live in it attack and utilize any foreign substance that is introduced and rapidly convert it into food, or dissolve it into its chemical components to become part of the salts in sea water.

Much care and maintenance must be bestowed upon these older wooden vessels or they are soon gone. It is a shame, because each one was made by hand, board by board, shaped and curved, sanded and planed by a true visionary artist. These men built a boat to work and to last, and quite often spent a year or two of their lives doing it.

They must have been extremely proud to see their boats catch the wind and perform as had been envisioned. In those days they worked without plans or drawings, and each boat was an individual, unique. Each builder had his own method, his own idea of perfection –resulting in boats that, though unique, were recognizable as his own creation.

A shallow draft is a tough proposition to build into a sailing vessel. Long heavy keels, short stout masts and a long boom, seem to be what worked the best for those times. They usually incorporated a notch in the transom, right in the center, that a long oar would fit into, which was used to scull the boat through the harbor or when there was no wind. There is an old saying around here that "There is a lot of water in Abaco, but in some places it is stretched mighty thin." In other parts of the world catamarans filled this shallow water need, but not here, all these boats were built for a more industrious group of mariners –they wanted to haul cargo to market, and lots of it.

The small wooden sailing dinghies are perhaps the most beautiful of all the boats present. Built for subsistence fishing and pleasure, they are still made on the island, in small numbers, as are the Albury motorboats. All of these show an old world craftsmanship and attention to detail not found anywhere else that I am aware of. Though beautiful to look at, every line and curve is there for a functional reason. They are built to be used, not looked at, and to me that gives them an even greater charm.

The harbor is not big enough for the largest yachts one sees in other places. These boats shine like new money and seem to personify the people who own them –flashy, arrogant, and fleeting. Though no doubt fun to be on, if one can afford it, these boats do not possess a soul in my opinion.

There are some of the larger sport fishing boats in evidence. Though the wind blows strongly during the winter months and most of the pelagic species of fish go further south, a few die-hards are here to go out and try on the better days. It is February right now and occasional dolphin can be had, but most of these guys are waiting for April. That is the time when the big runs of billfish, tuna, and wahoo are here.

A sport fishing boat is in a class alone –neither beauty nor beast. Though often shiny, they are built like the big workboats but with lots of specialized gear for the locating and capture of large fish. They are seaworthy too – they have to be. Tournaments are held in all weather, which means they will have to breast huge seas at times and maneuver faithfully while doing so. And then they need the power and range to go long distances and bring everyone back alive and on time. They can never have the looks of the classier sailing vessels or the raciness of the speedier powerboats, but they do have functionality and toughness. They do a job, and if done well, that can grant them a personality.

Many people all over the world are fascinated by boats as evidenced by the countless styles that occur. Every one of these is built a certain way to make it perform better at a certain task.

Take, for instance, the fan-tailed boats of Lafitte, Louisiana. These are magnificently beautiful masterpieces with broad sweeping decks and flowing lines. In most instances they are built at home, by the people intending to use them, and the fantail is not for looks. It is a clean, wide deck space for the hauling and working of a shrimp trawl. Interestingly, the design came about because of a tax levied on boats that was assessed proportionately to the length of the keel. A fantail just juts out over the water –no keel, no tax –rather ingenious, I'd say.

We won't get too deep into the purpose of the cigarette boats or other flashy speed boats –unless one is racing for legal, or, illegal reasons – they would seem to serve the same function as a red corvette, with a middle aged bachelor driving –only better. I have no personal experience as to their functionality – but they must work. There are a lot of them sold. A dear departed old friend of mine, Dun Mask, once made the profound statement that "Sex is the key driver of the entire world's economy." . . .think about it.

One does not have to be a shrimper, sponge diver, blue marlin fisherman or middle-aged bachelor to like boats. There are many kinds designed for average people and smaller jobs.

The most common inland variety is the jon-boat. Generally square fronted, sometimes pointed, they can be anywhere from eight to twenty feet or more long. Usually made out of aluminum, but not always, they are built to be lightweight, strong, and relatively inexpensive. They are the workhorses of the inland waters. Within this category specialization has created legions of sub-categories: flat bottom, v-hulls, tunnel hulls, work boats, fishing boats, fishing boats for various species –there is no one boat that will do it all and therein lies my fascination with boats. I love the ones that are good at what they do and marvel at the intricacies of design that made them so.

I have always collected boats. Never anything really big, though I would like to, and I have found truth in the old adage that says a man has two happiest days with a boat: the day he acquires it –all is joy and fulfillment; and the day he sells it –a sense of relief. This is correct for the reason I have already mentioned –no one boat will do it all.

Most of us have neither the storage space nor the money to get the perfect craft for everything we do or might want to do in the future. So, instead, we keep trading boats trying to find the "perfect one."

My own trading has proved true to form. I'm not counting jon-boats –I've bought enough of those, usually leaky, and usually at equipment auctions, to stock a dealership. It's kind of like puppies –I've never not come home with one that I went to look at. And pirogues don't count –everyone needs a few of those to leave at places. I seem to be financing an expansion down at the Go-Devil plant in Louisiana lately –but they are really well made and can technically be classified as jon-boats also. My greatest follies, besides maybe a few small sailboats, have been in the search for the perfect salt water fishing boat.

My perfect boat had to follow certain strict criteria: it had to be inexpensive- (that's a very relative term when dealing with boats); it had to be trailerable; it had to be low maintenance- (anyone who has owned a salt water boat is now choking with laughter); capable of carrying four people and enough fuel for a day; and safe in rough water; unsinkable wouldn't hurt and you can throw in pretty to boot.

My first love came to me in a most unusual manner. Jack Bellows, a man who I have known for many years, and trusted, a man who it turns out could sell a snake to a rat, came by my house on a beautiful spring day pulling a boat. He didn't say anything about the boat, just that he was looking for an old 870-pump shotgun and thought I might have one. Now, Mr. Bellows shoots Purdys, Foxes, stuff like that –and he is always trading them. I had actually been a victim on one or two of those trades –he was as sly as a Cheshire cat, and I knew it.

Like I said, he never mentioned the boat . . . but it was a beauty. Eighteen feet long with wide flaring bow –the kind of boat that you could picture slicing through the waves and sending white spray far out to the sides under a bright blue sky. It was a dark, cobalt blue, like deep water ... I was trying not to look at it and, like I said, he never mentioned it.

I found him an old 870, with all the bluing wore off, and put a magazine extension on it for him –he said he wanted it for home defense –and settled down to spit, whittle, and wait him out. Eventually, after we talked about turkeys, ducks ... anything but 870 shotguns or boats, he let slip that he might be up for a trade. I told him flat out that there was no way that my wife was going to put up with another boat... no way.

The first time that I used the boat we had a great cobia trip out of Dauphin Island. My hog hunting buddies, Charley and Chris, were with me and though we didn't have a clue what we were doing, we caught a bunch of fish. The boat performed perfectly and all was well. At the end of the day, while we were cleaning the catch from a dock, the boat sank. The motor was too heavy, and while sitting still for a period of time with water coming in through the scuppers, the bilge pump was overpowered. Live and learn.

Not possessed of unlimited resources, or much resources at all, we got her drained out and running again for the next trip. This time Robert Weaver and I went to Grand Isle for speckled trout. After a twelve-hour drive we put the boat in and took off for an evening try –eager to fish as it were. About two miles from the ramp the motor locked up . . . over-heated. A plastic bag floating in the water had wrapped perfectly over the water pump intake . . . more repairs.

Normally not superstitious, I sold the boat immediately – but the call of the sea had me by then.

The next love was a twenty-three foot Mako, about twenty years old –just in her prime – and she was a beauty. Nobody would call her a little girl –she was full figured in all the right places –but what graceful lines. I sent the paperwork in for her registration and immediately started an overhaul. She'd been used hard, but was built for it, and I'd have her ready in no time.

The FBI detective that soon showed up said there might be a delay – it was a stolen boat.

Eighteen months and several thousand dollars later she was mine again, but for some reason, not so shiny anymore. We made several trips with her and caught a lot of fish. She was big and heavy, which gave her a good ride, but in the end it led to her downfall.

The boat hung from the straps of a hoist over the water when not in use. It was a nice set-up, which allowed me to let the boat down and run it frequently without having to trailer anywhere. We had been gone for a couple of weeks and upon our return it was discovered that the back strap, which held up the most weight, had broken. The bow was still supported and this led to the complete inundation of the rear half of the boat, including the motor. It looked like it had been that way for a while because when I pulled it out of the water a nice flathead catfish was found living in the bilge.

I never could get the motor to work dependably after that and once again, it was time to move on.

A carefree peaceful year or so passed until my wife, Pumpkin, and I, found ourselves at a boat show in Florida on a cold, windy day in February. They had a little nineteen-foot Cape Horn that caught my eye –lightweight, indestructible we were told –it even had a brand new Honda motor! I believe in Honda, have had several of their products and encountered virtually no problems –and it was NEW!

It was a couple of years later when I learned a valuable lesson.

Pumpkin and I trailered the boat to Venice, Louisiana – one of our favorite places, not only for the fishing, but also for the scenery and bird life. My eldest daughter and soon-to-be son in law joined us. It was late in the day, not enough time to fish, but enough to take a cocktail cruise and show the kids the marsh. My plan was to head southeast out Baptist Collette to Breton Island, only a few miles into the gulf, and back for a nice dinner at the marina. We made it all the way down the pass and out into the gulf a couple of miles when the motor locked up. I could not figure out the problem and a north wind was kicking up –next stop Yucatan. No response on the radio and as the sun went down I gave up on starting the engine and began broadcasting a mayday. Once full darkness came it was easy to see there were boats out there, lights were everywhere! Why weren't they answering? And then it dawned on me, it was opening night of shrimp season –nobody was going to give up opening night to help some pleasure boaters.

An hour or so after dark the wind began to kick up a good bit and it looked like a rough night ahead. My calls on the radio became somewhat more convincing, apparently, until some poor sole who was spending the night on his boat after a hard day's fishing decided to answer. He wasn't planning to go back until the next day but he would tow us to the mouth of the pass, about five miles away, and leave us there. It would be a lot calmer, out of the wind, and if we didn't get a tow overnight he would be back by sometime the next day. We agreed wholeheartedly, were infinitely thankful, and so sorry for the inconvenience.

The good Samaritans had a large and powerful boat. Once secured with our anchor line (a tricky proposition in rough seas) they had no trouble planing out while towing our small boat. Constant steering was needed, on my part, or the boat could easily flip over in the rough seas. The spray coming over the bow was of such a volume that I could not read the GPS and it seemed that we had been traveling far too long. A quick glance at the sky revealed the North Star, and oddly, it was in the wrong place.

Yelling and waiving arms brought no response, but a quick call on the radio got them to stop and answer. Wafts of a strange smelling smoke drifted my way, sparking memories of youthful scenes of the seventies.

Still somewhat befuddled from the recent rough pounding, I tried to be as polite as possible, "Hey, uh... my GPS shows that we are headed to Gulfport."

Gulfport was over a hundred miles away, all open water, and this got their attention. There was silence, for a while, some fumbling around with a light... finally a very stoned sounding voice came back, "Ummm... yeh... We're havin a little trouble with our electronics. We'll start back out and you guide us on the radio... which way do we go?"

It was very late when we made it to the pass and our heroes decided to tow us all the way in – at least another fifteen miles –for which we were extremely thankful.

The very next time that boat went in the water it had two motors –live and learn.

Irma

A wise man once said to me that, "To each man, in a lifetime, is given one good woman, one great horse, and one great dog" . . . — Dr. Tom "Hoss" Morris, Coleman, Texas, 2008.

She first came into our lives a small white bundle of pure energy. Boney, ribs sticking out, she was the runt of the litter, but her spindly little legs seemed always to be in motion. Unlike most puppies, she was devoid of emotion –did not seem to crave attention or physical contact with human beings at all. She would not come when I called, ever, preferring to constantly run as if she even knew what she was searching for. The only way to get her back in her pen after a daily exercise run was to resort to some sort of trickery. Oh, and she learned fast.

At twelve weeks old she would hold point on any robins or blackbirds that happened to be walking around in the yard for as long as they would stay on the ground. The UPS guy, coming down the driveway on a delivery, commented on our beautiful English Pointer statue. That was Irma-Jean.

Once, thinking that it was high time for the pup to start paying attention to commands, I scolded her, mildly. She hid under the truck and I could not get my hands on her for a couple of days. Clearly, this dog required a light touch.

We had a few coveys of birds around the farm and whenever I happened to spot one it meant a quick dash to the kennel to get Irma. She had intensity, drive and range like I had never seen before, all she needed was a lot more bird contact – more than she could get around home.

I knew just who could remedy the situation – Harbert Muhlherin. Harbert, who lives in Dallas via Brownsville, Tennessee, is a guy who knows just about everybody in the country who could be called an avid bird hunter. He has trained dogs, traded dogs, run a quail preserve, Estanala—that is reputed to be one of the best in the country— and seems to have a job that involves mostly taking people hunting wherever the shooting is best anywhere on the planet. Harbert always has a couple of quail leases he is working on and an information network that lets him know in what part of the country the best hatches have occurred, what the chick survival was, and what the fall prospects should be.

My inquiry hit pay dirt. Apparently, South Texas had been too dry, Oklahoma had too much rain at the wrong time, but the West Texas area was going into the third year in a row of near perfect conditions. This was to be "the year of the quail," a once in a lifetime phenomenon – and he had a lease for me.

There were five of us that signed on to the lease, located near Coleman, Texas: Harbert, myself, and three gentlemen from the Crenshaw family –a renowned field trialing family out of Crenshaw, Mississippi. We had eight thousand acres of the poorest, roughest, thorniest land on earth – and it was full of quail. As with most Texas leases, this one was only available after deer season and so we settled in to wait until February.

Meanwhile, Irma terrorized the local bird population and even made a trip with me to North Dakota –the first time that I had ever set eyes on that country and a contributing factor to my move to that state a few years later. She was four months old at the time and pointed pheasants left and right, even on the windiest days in the windiest state in the nation. She and I killed a limit every day and even began to build a partnership. Though never outwardly affectionate, it was on this trip I learned that she needed me.

It was cold, and the wind bent the long grass over so that it rippled like a brown rug being shaken free of dust. Some snow, just about gone now, made everything wet and the little puppy probably didn't weigh twenty pounds. She was too little to carry a GPS collar, and was proving far too rangy and fast for me to be able to keep up with on foot. I tried to stay on high ground and catch glimpses of her from time to time, but she got away. Darkness was closing in and my whistling didn't seem to be penetrating the wall of wind. As I stood on the highest spot around, trying to decide whether to take shelter back at the truck or stick it out a little longer, she began to howl. It was the first noise of any kind that I had ever heard her make and I knew without doubt that it was she. The sound was the saddest, most emotional noise that I had ever heard a dog make. I understood it perfectly –she was lost, tired, cold, and wanted me to come get her. I finally found her in an area where the grass was several feet over her head –she was completely exhausted, could barely stand. I picked her up, carried her to the truck, and that night she slept on my bed. From that time forward she did a lot better at coming when called...mostly – except when she was hunting. No power on earth could make her stop when I was ready to go home.

It was December, a month and a half before our Texas lease would begin, when we finally struck a mutual agreement. I had been working on the command "Whoa!" for a while. She was getting it. Because of the fact that she would never quit hunting, I stumbled on the technique that we would use for the rest of her life. I simply carried a lead and when it was time to go, I'd let her pass nearby (hopefully), yell "Whoa!" and walk over to her and snap on the lead. Lots of praise ensued, which she ignored, but it worked! We were ready.

The Coleman ranch was hilly, sandy, and full of mesquite, prickly pear, cats-claw and wait-a-bit thorn. Oil-field roads criss-crossed in seemingly senseless patterns and a creek ran through the middle, making wheeled travel difficult at times. A few wild grasses along with some ragweed grew on the flat spots and these, along with mesquite beans, served as feed for the quail.

I hate getting flat tires, and the aforementioned thorn varieties were far too prevalent for me to risk my ride home, so we walked. Just crippled ole me and a six and a half month old puppy. I was only good for a couple of hours and on the first afternoon she found four coveys; the next morning it was five. We ran that afternoon but I had to call it off early –Irma looked like a bloody pincushion. She had thorns from her eyelids to her tail and down to the pads of her feet; despite my attempts at extraction, they just kept building up. On the eleven-hour ride home she slept on the front seat with her head in my lap –a first.

Five days rest and healing, and we were back in Texas. She learned how to get around without quite so many wounds; what had been an all-out race was now an elegant weave and hop. The only time she ever took off full bore was when a jackrabbit would challenge her to a race. How to stop this off-target activity puzzled me at first, until I realized that every time she took off on a race, she ended up on point –on a covey of quail. What the heck, maybe rabbits weren't all that bad.

By the fourth trip out west, she was finding seven to eight coveys per hunt and getting almost no thorns. By then she had completely taken over my sleeping bag and the front seat of the truck.

On our last visit to the Coleman ranch, my partners had been in there the week before and worked a lot of dogs. Coveys were scarce the first day and so Irma and I, by the light of a mesquite campfire, studied the ranch map. There seemed to be an area that had been overlooked. Some wading was involved, and a little hike to get there, but Irma was in complete agreement –we should try it.

Daylight brought a hard frost; temperature in the twenties and with some wind –poor scenting conditions by my reckoning, but it was the hand we'd been dealt. After a couple of miles to get in there, I let her off the lead, fresh, in a big grass and ragweed field. She took about twenty steps, and pointed... in the open. (That is a rare event, as those West Texas quail usually stick tight to heavy cover and thorns.) Anyway, a huge covey exploded and I knocked down a pair, which Irma helped to find. Though never much on the retrieve, I had out-stubborned her into at least helping me find the birds and it was beginning to pay off. When we came to the end of the ragweed, she had six finds in less than an hour. By noon she had found, and I had put up, twenty-two coveys –and she was still going strong.

We didn't have the Coleman lease the following year. As hard as it is to believe, there just weren't many birds in that part of the world –so goes the boom and bust cycles of quail populations in West Texas.

CRP was a young program at that time and we traveled around Mississippi and Arkansas a good bit. The birds were always widely scattered, but Irma could find them. Many times we ran a patch of CRP that the owners would say they had never seen a quail in –Irma would find a couple of coveys. Her instincts were so good, her technique so thorough, and nose so keen, that I honestly thought that if a covey was present, she would find it. Once or twice I was even so bold as to tell a landowner that he didn't have any quail, because Irma didn't find any.

Another year rolled by and Irma was now a grown-up dog. Her first year in Texas and the next rambling the South, had taught her a lot and given her quite a reputation among those who had seen her in action. We received an invitation to hunt on my good friend Jack Stokes' quail plantation in Holly Springs, Mississippi. It was a place that he had put a lot of work into and was reputed to be full of birds. The weather was cool that day and we were finding plenty of quail, but after an hour and a half Irma came back to the wagon and wanted to be put up . . .

I took her to the vet the very next day; she had no outward signs of trouble, but I knew something was wrong –X-rays showed the problem…heartworms.

I was sick – the vet tried to tell me that I must have missed an application of heartworm medicine –I told him he was wrong and maybe the medicine was no good.

She was treated for heartworms, a procedure that nearly kills the dog in itself, and sent home for rest and recuperation. Everything seemed to be fine until about four months later, when she died overnight. A blood clot, left over from the heartworm infestation, had lodged in her lung.

I did a little research on the heartworm medicines and soon came to the conclusion that Ivermectin based medicines had been in use exclusively, for so long, that the heartworm populations in certain areas had built up resistance. When I alerted several veterinarians to this fact they at first did not believe me, but within a few months it became general knowledge and new preventatives began to appear that did not use Ivermectin. I only wish that it could have happened just a little sooner.

If a man is truly lucky in life, he can hope to have: one good woman, one great horse, and one great dog. Cherish them while you can.

Every Dog Has His Day

The Wirehaired Pointing Griffon is a breed of dog along the lines of a multi-purpose hunting dog. German by decent, as most multi-purpose breeds are these days, they are supposed to find, point, track, retrieve, guard the game, guard the house, and exhibit a rare and keen intelligence while doing it. Their coat is wiry, as the name implies, and is touted to protect them in all environments and weather extremes. It is also said to be hypoallergenic.

I don't believe my dad had ever had a dog before. I had dogs and the family had dogs, but Daddy never really had one of his own. I'm sure it was the empty nest syndrome that came when my sister and I both went off to school.

As always, Dad did his research, and was intrigued by the Griffons. He ordered one from someplace far away, specifying a male, and Arthur showed up at Memphis International Airport.

Bushy-browed like my dad, leggy, stub-tailed, his deep brown eyes could look all the way through you as if he were watching events unfold in a faraway land. Maybe he was.

Aside from physically getting bigger, Arthur didn't change any. He seemed to be mentally mature at twelve weeks. Aloof with strangers, affectionate with family, he was content to be at his master's side—unless whatever Dad wanted him to do was beneath his dignity, like mindless repetitive retrieving or sitting still in a dove field. Arthur seemed to make his own decisions as far as hunting and retrieving were concerned.

Dad's hunting club, Hatchie Coon, each year prepared a large and heavily baited dove field, as was the custom at that time. For the first few weekends in September the membership and guests would gather for some fast and furious shooting—followed by good BBQ and fellowship. On that particular year, Dad planned to debut Arthur and show everyone what a true gun dog looked like.

Opening day arrived and there was a big gathering. It was to be a shotgun start at two p.m.—the traditional way at Hatchie Coon. All participants were lined up, in their vehicles in front of the clubhouse, engines revving and jockeying for position. At the appointed minute the club president, Scott May, fired a gun and the mile long race was on– to the dove field and also to claim a choice position. Dad stayed behind to let the dust settle while I raced with the pack.

I managed to stake out a piece of territory on the far side of the field and was immediately busy. A thirty-acre field with fifty guns going off does some strange things to a dove's psychology; consequently the bird to shell ratio goes way down—at least, that is my excuse.

I probably had five or six birds when Arthur passed by the first time. He had a really nice gate and was showing excellent stamina, even in the heat. The bird I had just shot bounced right in front of him and he caught it on the fly and was gone. OK, so I get to shoot another—no big deal. A few minutes later he came by again and helped someone else—wow, that dog could really cover some ground!

Over the course of the afternoon I was able to critique Arthur's range and scenting capabilities many times. I lost a couple more doves to him, but he did not single me out by any means. When I found Daddy, at quitting time, he looked red faced and worn.

"How's he doing Daddy?" I asked, feigning optimism.

"Not so well... I believe he went quail hunting... somewhere."

Glancing around, I took in a good sized pile of birds but very few spent hulls; this sort of thing requires great delicacy, and I knew it, so it was with some caution that I asked, "which way did he go?"

"Out, I don't know. He breezes by here every now and then and leaves a bird."

"Maybe you should tie him up?"

He looked at me with the coldest eyes I had ever seen him make, "He has broken two ropes and now won't come when I call."

"...OH..."

Arthur's training continued with varying degrees of success. Dove shooting in a crowded environment was not his thing. Daddy tried ropes and shock collars, but at heart, Arthur was a seeker— he liked quail and running. Often over the first year or two Arthur was seen dashing across a field, long lead rope trailing and a cooler or chair bouncing along behind. Several times I was cornered by the host of an upcoming, invitation-only dove shoot and surreptitiously asked, "Are ya'll coming...good, good... Uh, is your dad going to bring that... what kind of dog is that again?"

All I could say was, "I'm sure he will." Daddy and Arthur were inseparable, and besides, dogs don't get better by being left at home—Daddy was not the type to give up on any of his children.

During quail hunts Arthur was more in his element. Somewhat rangy for the breed, he did, at least, look for something to point. He pointed all sorts of things, some of which were quail, and Dad and I shot a bird or two over him on occasion.

It is an unwritten rule that one should never speak ill of another's dog, at least in his presence. Wives and children do not fully have this protection nor do bosses or presidents. My father, God rest his soul, is no longer with us and Arthur predeceased him by a few years, therefore I can now say, without breaking the code and with some generosity, that Arthur was a mediocre hunter with a mediocre nose. Be that as it may, no dog's star shines brightly on every trip afield, but, as the saying goes...

A cold, biting wind whipped around the sidewalls of the twenty-foot Polar cab boat. Fine spray, sliced from the crests of waves and then driven into the windshield and roof, found ways to pool together into good sized droplets and then work its way through the seams and into the interior. Inside this interior space, and huddled as far forward as possible so as to be less accessible to the majority of these annoyances, rode four men and a dog. That is, if men can be defined by size or the ability to vote and go to war.

John Stokes, the owner of the boat, was explaining our course of action to my dad. "The island is called Sunrise and I've leased it from Westvaco Timber Company for many years. There is a lot of game on it, all kinds: turkey huntin' is excellent," his eyes took on a reminiscent gleam before continuing, "there are some really big deer, lots of hogs—I think Charley Lowrance had something to do with that—an' good duck huntn' when the river's right. The boys," that would be Jack and me, "know the island perty good, and what we are gonna do is line up and go through the big plum thicket. It's on the highest ground and supposedly has a lot of quail. Does that dog… I can't remember what he's called… does he point quail?"

My dad, in his med-school precise teaching voice began, "Arthur is a Wire Haired Pointing Griffon of the finest bloodlines. He points all types of game." He was warming to his subject "The first Duke of…"

"What about rabbits?" Mr. John had to know, "Some people don't like rabbits shot in front of their bird dogs."

"Griffons are multi-purpose dogs bred to adapt to all types of game. You may shoot anything in front of Arthur."

I could tell that Mr. John, somewhat outspoken at times, was skeptical of Arthur's usefulness on our adventure, but he politely withheld further comment.

As the big, high, square bowed boat squeezed between the willows and nudged onto the muddy bank, Jack jumped off the bow with a stout line and made fast to a suitable tree. Arthur followed, took ten steps and then froze on point. His points weren't classy, he had almost no tail—didn't lift a paw or anything, he just stopped moving. The rest of us were unloading and organizing for the upcoming trek.

"Hey, what's that dog doing?" Mr. John wanted to know.

Dad looked out around the side of the boat and said, "pointing," in a matter-of-fact tone.

"Well golly-darn, there can't be anything right there on the bank! We could see it if there was."

With complete confidence Dad just said "Arthur scents game."

John, gun in hand and still struggling to put on his shell vest, scrambled over the bow and walked over to the dog— "There's nothing here!" he called back.

Arthur never moved.

Jack and I watched from fifteen feet away. Arthur was looking at a log that had floated up on the bank. John walked around the log a couple of times, kicked it, and then tried to peer inside one end.

"There's nothing here, lets get going!" proclaimed our host.

We all started up the bank but Arthur wouldn't move. Daddy called, Arthur stayed where he was.

"He has game there," says my dad, certain of it.

Exasperated, Mr. John proclaimed that there couldn't be, as he marched back over to the log and gave it a mighty stomp.

The log, after untold years of alternately floating down the river and resting on its banks, had finally become somewhat decayed. Mr. John's foot went through the outer part and into the hollow interior. This was immediately followed by a terrible screeching sound as a jumbo raccoon shot out and attempted to climb the nearest object—Mr. John's leg. Before Mr. Coon could get very high up, Arthur's jaws had closed on his neck and a lively battle ensued, with Mr. John dancing around and cheering for his new favorite dog.

BBQ'd coon is a southern delicacy and I threw the fat, fifteen-pounder up on the bow and hurried to catch up with the rest of the party. Arthur did not come with us, he was still back at the log, pointing.

"Hey Dad, call Arthur, he won't leave the log," I yelled.

Daddy called, but Arthur wouldn't budge. "I'll go back and lead him for a while," says my father, "He is still smelling that coon."

By then Mr. John was on his way back down the riverbank, "Hold on a minute! I believe him!" as he hustled over to the site.

Arthur just stood there, with his stubby little tail barely wiggling.

A few kicks on the log brought no response; there didn't seem to be any more soft spots and nothing could be seen by peering into the end. A stout limb was soon procured and put to work as a pry-bar. Once this was inserted into the hole and leaned on, a loud crack was heard and a big piece of the log broke away. Another coon came bolting out and met a charge of number eight shot from Mr. John's Browning.

At this point Jack's dad was ecstatic, "I love that dog!" he raved, "Where can I get one of those?"

Daddy just beamed, as happy as a dog owner can ever be.

Just up the bank and well before the plum thicket, the willows gave way to a predominately cottonwood forest. At the junction, the transition zone between the two plant communities where older willow is infiltrated by younger cottonwood, Arthur pointed again. When the bird got up, we were surprised and delighted to see that it was a woodcock, a rare prize for us and a uniquely beautiful bird with excellent culinary attributes. A few yards later there was another… and another after that.

We stayed in this transition zone for a good while and Arthur ranged back and forth in front of our skirmish line and pointed woodcock seemingly every few yards. As if he were showing off, he

even managed to tree a couple of red squirrels and a possum—
our vests were getting heavy and so the possum was left alone.

Eventually, we made it out into the open, sandy country
known as the plum thicket. With poor to no top soil, this area
had an entirely different plant community: plum bushes, with
roots that could go and find water, and some fast growing,
sparse grasses that could make it on just a rain or two made
up the bulk of the ecosystem. For some unknown reason
quail thrived there where nothing else could.

It was a vast area, mostly open sand and dense clumps of
thorny plums, and Arthur took to it like it was his everyday fare.
At a steady lope, he covered the ground by passing downwind
of every thicket on our rout. The area encompassed about
one hundred and fifty acres or so, and Arthur found the first
covey of quail, a big one, within the first hundred yards. By
the time we had gone down one side he had found six more
and every thicket out there had birds in it; if not a fresh covey,
then singles or pairs that we had already flushed.

No one had more than a shell or two left by then, and
the short winter sun was casting long shadows under the
cottonwoods. There was no objection when Mr. John
suggested we head back—save this spot for another day. Our
shooting vests were chock full of quail and woodcock, as well
as two big fox squirrels, several rabbits, and, of course, the
two jumbo coons back at the boat—it was a day such that no
one with a hunters soul could ever forget, especially my dad.

And lastly, but most importantly, there was total conviction
in our minds, that no dog, anywhere, ever, did a better job
than Arthur did that day. It just goes to show you–every dog
has his day!

Flood

The year 2011 will be remembered by many as the year of the great floods. We who live along the mighty Mississippi are no virgins when it comes to high water inundations, but this was different. Many millions of dollars were lost, unavoidably, because of the severity of the flood. Many millions more were lost due to bureaucratic incompetence. Let's hope that we can learn from our mistakes.

Throughout history catastrophic flooding has occurred regularly and our government has spent trillions of our tax dollars to stop it. Flood control projects have had some success and surely save lives and money on a regular basis, but usually have negative impacts on ecology and the environment. Flood plains, by definition, need floods to sustain their stated character and fertility. Nature is, by definition, natural, and we change this at our own peril.

Before the white man came to North America the Mississippi River flooded vast tracts of the Delta and adjacent bottomlands annually, leaving layer after layer of sediment to become some of the richest farmland in the world. The indigenous people of that era knew enough to stay out of its way, or build a few mounds to wait out a flood. These events were surely expected as the natural order of things, rather than as a natural disaster. When Hernando Desoto first camped near what would become Memphis, in the year 1543, he encountered a flood that lasted for forty days. It was not a big deal, he knew it would subside. It was only after civilization gained a foothold on the continent that flooding became a problem.

In the winter of 1734 and into the spring of 1735, the city of New Orleans was inundated for several months, causing great loss and hardship and also causing much debate as to the wisdom of remaining at that location. By the mid 1800's, private landowners had built a series of levees all along the lower Mississippi to protect their financial investments. Between 1858 and 1900 there were more than a dozen major flooding events, which breached and destroyed portions of this system.

The flood of 1927, sometimes called "The Great Flood," is still considered one of the costliest natural disasters in human history. By that time man had walled in the mighty Mississippi for good, it was believed, and human optimism led many to invest in projects within the floodplain. As usual, Mother Nature proved that she has neither boundaries nor limits and topped all previous records by a wide margin. The levees at Caernaroon, Louisiana, fourteen miles below New Orleans, were dynamited to save the city. As a result, St.

Bernard and Plaquemines Parish were flooded. My guess is that the farmers down there did not vote for the dynamiting. Elsewhere, the river came over the tops of the existing levees all up and down the entire system.

Public outcry after this event was so great that the then commerce secretary, Herbert Hoover, introduced legislation to "gain control of the river once and for all." This led to the Flood Control Act of 1928 and the placement of the U.S. Army Corps of Engineers in charge. Massive investments in dams, reservoirs, levees and spillways were made, and the Yazoo Mississippi Delta Levee Board was asked to maintain the "Great Levee" along a ninety-eight mile stretch located just south of Memphis, Tennessee. All seemed reasonably well with the world until 1937, when the river topped even the "Great Levee"— which then had to be raised. When this was accomplished everyone was told that no flood could breach this man-made marvel... until 2011.

Heavy spring rains along the Ohio River valley that year, coupled with the prospect of above average snow melt, were making the river forecasts alarming for those of us who farm along the Mississippi. The river had risen to twenty-four feet on the Memphis gauge by March first. My farm, seventy miles to the south, was only a day's flow away. Flood stage in Memphis starts at thirty-four feet, a devastating level for most of us, and the forecasts were inching up in that direction. Half of my farm is behind the levee and previous floods had taught me the value of risk management. Everything back there was now either bottomland forest or CRP. This absence of cropland did not completely do away with flood risk; I still had a camp house –built eight feet above ground and located on a high ridge –and a well, likewise perched on a ridge and a man- made mound. Both house and well had seen many a flood with never a close call. My main worry was for the timber and wildlife –both of which I could do nothing about.

On March fifth my access road to the bature land went under. I did not see this road again until nearly July.

Toward the end of March, we seemed to have a crest; thirty-six feet in Memphis, two feet over flood stage, but still plenty of ridge tops showing. The deer, turkey and other denizens of the forest were somewhat bunched up, a stressful situation no doubt, but not lethal. It appeared that all would be well when the water level subsided about eight feet over the next week, as forecast. Maybe we would have a normal year after all.

Sometime around then the snow-pack in the Rocky Mountains, two hundred and twelve percent of normal volume, began to get into the Missouri River. The Ohio was still flooding and the Corn Belt was getting heavy rains repeatedly. Next, Eastern Montana received an entire year's worth of rainfall in one month –all adding to the Missouri flooding and heading my way.

The forecasts began to jump, as did the Mississippi. We were now looking at the possibility of a flood the likes of which no living person had ever seen.

Up and down the river landowners and hunting club members began making plans to empty their cabins and remove all equipment from the previously deemed safe places. In most cases, because of the ridgey topography of the lands bordering the Mississippi, the rescuers had to wait until the river got really high before going in with suitably large boats capable of carrying out all of their belongings. The big boats can't go through the flooded woods and were necessarily confined to existing roads, which usually follow the ridge tops.

It was at this time that the Levee Board, the group that we taxpayers fund to manage the levee, declared that no one could cross or set foot on it. Hundreds of property owners were summarily denied access to their own private property in a time of dire need.

Many of us defied orders and found a way in. Some were arrested. No reasons were given other than that we would get in the way of Levee Board operations.

Knowing that this was an illegal denial of access, I visually ascertained that no particular operations were being performed on my leased portion of levee, and called the Clarksdale, Mississippi, office to get permission to launch a boat from my road as it came across the levee.

After a few minutes on hold, the head guy came on the line –"Buck, I just can't let you guys get in the way of my equipment."

I explained to him where my farm was and that there had been no equipment, within sight or hearing, in the last two weeks; all I was asking for was permission to back a boat down my private gravel road, out of the way – and in case some flurry of activity was planned, I even offered to park the truck and trailer across the levee in my cotton field.

"You !#% farmers up and down this river knew !#%* well this was coming and should have been ready before now! I'm not letting anybody set foot on that levee. You should have gotten your !@#% stuff out before now!"

I hung up, stunned. I had just been told that I was an idiot for not knowing the river would get this high by a man that did not know it either; that I could not have access to my own property by a man that had no right to deny it; and that I should have gone in earlier by a man that was obviously unaware of the terrain problems ubiquitous to the entire river system that he was managing . . . interesting.

On May the seventh we had a river crest of forty-three point eight-three feet at Memphis, almost thirteen feet above flood stage and near the record set in 1927 of forty-eight point seven. The Levee Board did not let anyone have access across the levee until June and the river remained high enough to cover some roads and flood most low areas until the middle of July.

I drove a boat, illegally, by my camp several times during the flood. The house, built on telephone poles, had five feet of water inside for several weeks. I had parked a four-wheeler on the mound at the wellhead, and tied it to the engine block of the power unit with about eight feet of stout line. It floated at first, but was eventually pulled under and ruined. I drained the diesel power unit and gear head, replaced all fluids etc., and it is currently functioning. The camp house is a solar-powered/cordwood constructed building with interior walls that were made of straw bales plastered with mud stucco. Straw bales turned out to be less than ideal in a flood, otherwise I was fairly lucky.

Others were not nearly so. The land behind the levee in this area is mostly forested, sometimes several miles wide, and composed of a series of hunting clubs. Many of these clubs have some high ground or an old levee where the members build cabins or even houses, mostly for recreational use. My brother-in-law has one of these on an old-levee spur about twenty miles south of my farm. The club is called Ward Lake and is one of the premier, well-run, hunting clubs along the river. There are several dozen houses on this property and the club next to it, and they all went at least partially under water. When I joined the first wave of people "allowed" back there, June 1, eight a.m., I was astounded by the devastation. My job as volunteer was to wash several inches of clay sediment off of everything on the insides of several houses with a Honda pump and fire hose. I found guns, laptop computers, telephones, TV's, furniture… the list goes on. All of this stuff could easily have been loaded onto even smaller craft and ferried out well before going under. The club is one with many affluent members. Several of them are lawyers. The litigious type. My guess is that the powers of the levee board will be limited to a more reasonable, common sense level, in the future.

As soon as this clean up was over, I headed to the ranch in North Dakota. The aforementioned Missouri River was still flooding in Iowa and Missouri, causing some major detours. Bismarck, North Dakota was even experiencing flooding and my good friend Dave Shockman called me for some input on what he should do to his house; the new flood forecast now encompassed his whole neighborhood.

"Surely you guys can pool your money and put up a levee somewhere? There are a lot of really nice houses around there."

"Well, I thought so too," said Dave, "but when these huge earth movers showed up and started putting up a giant wall of dirt, I knew that I was in real trouble."

"How come? It might work."

"When they started building it, I realized that my house was on the wrong side."

". . . Oh."

Seems like other people were having trouble with government agencies also.

The Yazoo Mississippi Delta Levee Board does a fine job of maintaining its section of levee and associated interior drainage projects. This is their stated mission, and I, for one, am glad to have them do it. No government agency should have the unlimited authority to mandate whatever rules it likes, especially when such rules trample the constitutional rights of individuals. In this country, private property ownership is a right we all have. Access to same is mandated by law. Another great flood will come; an even bigger one I'm sure –but maybe not in my lifetime. Future generations beware – do not let too much government intervention into your lives – it will come back to bite you!

"The Boars Den". This cabin sits on a high ridge and eight feet in the air on telephone poles.

A Picture is Worth?

A cold wind blew ripples out of the darkness across the flooded road. Headlights, now covered in soupy mud, only vaguely illuminated the course and direction we needed to go. Tractor ruts, now holding the old Chevy Blazer in line, were the only indications of veracity and all four wheels pulling together and outfitted with Co-op Grip Spurs were needed this morning. Four a.m. is a lonely time to get stuck on a backcountry gravel road in Arkansas.

It was January third, 1980, and Clayton George and I were headed to the Bayou de View club, by invitation, for a duck hunt in the famous big-timbered bottoms. Hank Mchorris and Allen Hughes were our hosts, and anxiously awaited our arrival from the comfortable confines of the old clubhouse with the gigantic, ever-in-use, oak burning fireplace.

Recent rains had been heavy, causing the bayou to rise and flood the vast bottoms. A following cold front served to skim-ice the fields and to push the ducks into the shelter of the big timber. The conditions were ideal for ducks, but these same rains had flooded the roads going in and then the water had frozen in the ruts. It was causing me to be late, a condition that tends to introduce panic into my psychological profile—at least as far as duck hunting goes. Thirty minutes early is the unwritten rule for avid duck hunters… We were barely going to be on time.

Hank is the huntmaster at the Bayou de View. He spends a lot of time observing and has an uncanny knack of predicting what the birds are going to do on any given day. There was only one other group of hunters present that morning at the club, and Hank gave them first choice of shooting locations, with probably a little bit of skillful manipulation involved. They chose Big Lake, a well known and proven location, and Hank shuttled them out the door and on their way; when he came back in he had a big grin on his face—"It's Little Lake for us!" he proclaimed with a fist pump or two, "I've already got a boat and motor at the landing that I forgot to tell them about—so let's go!"

We loaded our gear into the Blazer and all four of us, along with Lady, my Labrador, climbed in. A short drive to a locked gate and another half mile beyond brought us to the secluded landing on the bayou. Tall cane surrounded us for several hundred yards and blocked enough of the wind to make it quite pleasant, and peaceful. Looking out from the landing place the dark waters of the bayou ran swiftly by with barely a whisper while wind gusts periodically built up to a low moan in the tops of the giant cypress and tupelo; wood ducks squealed in the darkness and wing beats accompanied by low murmurs told of other unseen stirrings above. In the occasional silence, the barred owl held raucous court over all the miles of flooded bottom.

Every club seems to have its own type of preferred boat and this one used a type of flat bottomed craft called a Buddy Boat: light weight, narrow, low-slung, it is the perfect boat to skull from the front while bream fishing on a warm summer day. It is also the tippiest, lowest, leakiest form of aquatic transportation in the state of Arkansas. The only saving grace is that it *is* very narrow; as in narrow enough to get between the trees and knees in the torturous, twisting channels that one must thread throughout the bayou.

The three passengers and dog lay down in the bottom and hoped for the best, while Hank, declining the offer of a light, bumped, ground, and glanced his way through seemingly invisible trails in the forest.

There was just a hint of daylight in the east when we came to a long, narrow, opening that our guide announced was Little Lake. As if on cue, mallards erupted on all sides and the graying sky above seemed to be full of them –all looking as if they wanted down in the timber. It appeared that Hank had made a fair choice, I thought.

He explained the set up: the water was too deep to wade and we were not all going to be in one blind; rather, there were three stands, all on the east side and situated some fifty or so yards apart. I was to take the first stand, which was the last one on the downstream end, and Lady was to do pick up duty for everyone from there; the middle went to Clayton and Allen, and the north end would be Hank. The plan was to let the ducks come all the way down into the timber, and, with the wind strong out of the north, they were naturally going to pile into the north end of the lake. Hank was to shoot the last duck, before it lit, thus scaring the rest of the flock back down the lake and past the other blinds, hopefully before they could gain enough altitude to escape out of the tall-timbered sides.

My blind was simply a three by four foot platform built between a couple of cypress trunks, with a bench on one end. A couple of inches of water covered the floor and so any items that needed to be kept dry went on the bench, along with my duck bucket.

Perhaps a word is in order about the duck bucket. Duck buckets of that era were generally made out of metal trash cans, sixteen or so inches tall, and with the top beaten down into the shape of a seat– the whole thing then painted camo. They held the keys to feast or famine, comfort or adversity, sometimes even life or death: dry socks, fire building material, extra gloves, food, compass, shells, calls—anything and everything that might be needed on an all-day hunt or in an emergency—and unlike today's "blind bags," you could sit on them comfortably.

Thus, with everything stowed away in its proper place, it was time to enjoy the show. Just about everyone in the group was handy with a duck call, or at least thought they were, and soon the birds began to really pile into the lake. Lady and I watched as small groups of contented mallards preened and splashed, slowly drifting past us on the current; occasional groups would form into wavy lines in a follow-the-leader sort of way and then wind their way back into the dark timber where the omnipresent wood ducks splashed and squealed in gleeful abandon. Every few minutes, another raucous group of mallards would come down from above with a roar of wings, chattering, quacking and adding to the general confusion.

The order to take the next bunch was passed down stream and Lady, a one year old, perked up in expectation when I began shoving shells into the old pump gun. Bird watching was just not her thing.

Within minutes a large group of mallards ducked down below the timber right in front of us and it was all Lady and I could do to restrain ourselves. True to plan, a rarity, they continued on up the lake and settled into the north end. I could not see up that way, but the shots that began told the story and it sounded like it was headed my way. Crouching, ready, the remnants showed up a few seconds later— not quite at tree top level— and a pair of drakes fell over on the far side. Lady was just about halfway back with our first customer when the up-streamer's bag began to float by; my second bird had hung up on a stob and so I sent her for a hen that was already getting below us – several more ducks floated by and some more shooting, Lady was getting a real workout now—more shots were fired, and a few of my own…

When Hank came to pick me up an hour later I was frantic, "Lady couldn't keep up! I don't know how many ducks got by us, maybe ten or more!"

Hank was not worried. "We hunt here all the time with no dog and there are a couple of logs down below that will catch them."

I wished I had known. Lady and I had ducks piled on every available surface and barely had room to stand on the platform. "Oh…good," was all that I could think of.

We headed down stream and sure enough, eleven fat mallards were caught on the strategically placed retrieving logs.

It was only eight o'clock, and instead of going in, our hosts decided that we should clean a few birds on a ridge further back in the bottoms. Our arrival at a beautiful oak ridge was followed by fire making and a duck cleaning detail; Clayton then decided that he was hungry, not at all an unusual condition for him in those days, and offered to cook a few ducks for our breakfast. Enough salt, pepper, bacon, and Coca-Cola was scavenged out of our duck buckets to put on quite a feast and he got right down to it. Later, because the sun shown so brightly and we were all very full, and because it was a most picturesque spot and we were all extremely content, naps were in order.

It was nearly eleven when we decided to head back, and because the water was rising, we had picked up the decoys at Little Lake and had quite a load. Hank took Allen, a limit of greenheads and the decoys, out on the first trip. He then returned and picked up Clayton and me, along with the rest of the ducks. We had something less than a limit— all greenheads— proudly displayed on the front of the boat, along with the remainder of the breasted ducks which were hidden in Clayton's duck bucket.

Just as the boat touched the landing, a green-clad Arkansas Game and Fish Department field officer jumped out of the cane, and another– two game wardens; one of them the famous local warden in a very tough area who had the reputation of being very, very, strict. These men had walked a long way and hid a very long time to check us, they probably would have rather been somewhere else right then, as had we.

After checking our guns, licenses, and ducks, the younger one, possibly in an effort to be cordial, but more likely as a means of obtaining information, said "You boys shore did a lot of shootin this morning!"

Hank replied with as much modesty as he could muster, "Well, we're not very good shots."

My eyes started feeling drawn to Clayton's bucket, but I fought them away with a great effort. It appeared to me that the bucket was glowing, slightly, and maybe even vibrating a little—how could they not see it?

"I figured you guys were OK," he said, "You quit shooting mighty early."

Thank goodness, I thought.

The older man told the other to help us unload the boat so we could all ride out of there, and the first thing he grabbed was the glowing bucket.

Clayton said, "I can get that."

"Got it," says the strong young warden and with the other hand he grabbed a decoy bag for the short trek up the bank, Clayton right on his heels. "Shore is heavy," he commented, "What all you got in here?"

"Shells... and my camera," says Clayton, thoughtfully.

I saw it coming, right then. I wanted to tackle Clayton but there was no way to stop him now.

"Umm, do you guys mind if I get a picture?" says he.

"Sure, if ya'll can give us a ride out, we have some more stops to make today."

Clayton lined the two wardens up on each side of the tailgate with a big pile of neatly arranged ducks between them... and the now shrieking bucket, and took the picture.

I could have killed him.

L-R, The author, Hank, Clayton George— cooking.
Allen Hughes is the photographer.
Bayou De view, January 3, 1980

Ice Fishing?

To the southern angler the term *fishing* invokes memories of sun-filled days spent drifting about on tranquil waters. The birds are singing and turtles bask in the warmth of the sun. Occasionally a snake will swim by and, if it gets cloudy or late in the day, bullfrogs will start up with their booming chorus emanating from the shaded shallows. Fish splash, from time to time, or try to take your offering, but it is difficult to remain alert for any length of time… it is just too comfortable.

From March through November southern anglers go fishing whenever they want; the other three months are available, for sure, but everyone needs a break sometime, and besides, it can get chilly then.

Northern anglers are less fortunate; they get just a few months to fish in a Christian manner before the surface of the water freezes. Once this happens, it will usually remain that way until the spring thaw. Shorter and shorter days exhibit progressively fewer hours of rapidly weakening sunlight. Soon the cold winds blow drifting snow across a landscape devoid of distinction between land and water. Sunlight is then reflected back into space, where it does no good, and the dreaded Old Man Winter is now buckled-up for the long ride.

In my experience, Yankees are a hardy bunch and industrious to boot. They have found a way to fish when there is no fishing to be had and the method they use is called "ice fishing." It is fairly common the further you go north, and has all of it's own gear, methods, conveyances and gizzwizzes— a veritable boon to the economy in sporting goods sales.

Why this happens is a puzzlement to me. I have been ice fishing, once, and can only describe the process as the purest, most distilled form, of unadulterated misery. Furthermore, it is my hypothesis that it is only performed at all, or at least on a regular basis, by people who are completely deprived of anything else to do— people need regular doses of sunlight for proper mental acuity. At any rate, it is big business up north, stimulates the economy to some degree and occupies a portion of the population that would be up to no telling what if they couldn't fish.

As you might have guessed, ice fishing is not a sport for which I can profess any degree of expertise. Furthermore, it is an unusual subject for discussion in my house— but somehow we were on it, Dave Shockman and I. Now, Dave is an avid outdoorsman— great wing-shot, savvy dog-man, does it all— but most of his expertise centers around guns, or bows. Judging by his fishing gear— always in a tangled state of disrepair—I didn't see him as someone who would put out a whole lot of effort to catch a fish. Especially a fish through a hole in the ice. He was trying to tell me how much fun it was... etc. etc...blah-blah, and my mind kept putting up images and memories for review that were, to put it mildly, unpleasant. Thinking to add to my store of negative knowledge, I asked him if he had ever had any mishaps— dangerous situations or accidents— while ice fishing. Or was it always just dull, and cold. He thought about this for a minute or so, mentioned that the ice sometimes sagged, forcing water onto the surface via the holes chopped through it— this could ruin a pickup truck if one didn't move quickly enough— but this was a common occurrence; or maybe the time the ice broke apart while he was on it— drifting off into oblivion— but once again, these were just common mishaps, not really worth mentioning. But then his face took on that faraway look of remembrance, and I could tell that he was on to something. Something big. A moment later he refocused in my direction and asked, in a matter-of-fact sort of way, "Do you want me to tell you about the ice fishing trip from hell?"

Who could resist that?

In preparation, Dave got up and poured another Coke and then settled himself in Granny Buckingham's old rocker— the one with the uncomfortably rounded back that I had inherited, somehow, and for some unknown reason hauled all the way from Mississippi to North Dakota. Leaning back, and with his feet up on the footstool, he could see a vast expanse of prairie out of the front window and hear the incessant wind, though faintly, that bent the prairie grasses. On the horizon geese traded back and forth to the big lake that we called Latawata and normally they would have had his full attention, but this time they did not. He was looking a lot farther away than that— his mind was searching deep into the mists of time…

He began… "In January, 1992, North Dakota was experiencing an exceptionally cold winter. Night-time temperatures were getting to twenty below or better and the snow was deep and wasn't going to be melting any time soon. My two brothers, Peter and Steve, and a friend named Buddy — you don't know him but we used to get in a lot of trouble together— we decided to go ice fishing up north. Since we live in North Dakota, up north means Canada— like three hundred and fifty miles north of Winnipeg. The lake was one that we had fished in summer, and it had some really big walleyes in it. We thought that winter fishing should be even better, and easier. You see, there is not a whole hell of a lot to do up here in winter. It didn't matter that it was January, or that a cold front was coming in, we were North Dakotans and we were used to it, young and invincible.

We loaded up my Suburban and a big trailer with all the gear we might need: a diesel generator, three hundred gallons of diesel fuel, two hundred and fifty gallons of gasoline, four snowmobiles, two portable ice fishing shelters, fishing gear, and a little food— mostly we would eat what we caught. We left Berlin, North Dakota, early on a Wednesday and drove to Winnipeg and then 100 miles further north on a good road— meaning it was plowed regularly— with no problems. The final two hundred and fifty miles to the lodge where we were going to stay was on a *winter road* — which means it was not plowed very often. We decided to push straight through. The road was so rough that our top speed was maybe ten miles per hour. It took us twenty-seven hours to go that two hundred and fifty miles.

When we got to the lodge it was midnight. They had no record of our reservation. There were no rooms available due to construction work in the area and the temperature was sixty degrees below zero. We told them we would take anything, anywhere, and they rented us a storage shed with plywood walls. It cost us two hundred a night and came with wood for a heater, but we had to chop it first— they supplied an axe. The cost of a beer was ten dollars and a bottle of whiskey was set at three hundred and seventy-five. Gasoline was nine dollars a gallon. If we had any sense we would have returned home the next day, but we didn't.

The lake we were going to fish, the fabulous lake with the big walleyes, was another sixty miles away via snowmobile. I got up the next morning, ready to fish, and went out to warm up the machines. When I pulled the chord on the first one, the entire dashboard exploded. Not one of the three others would start either and it took us a day and a half to get them running. We had now spent over three days of our seven day trip and had not fished one minute. It started to dawn on us that maybe we were in a little over our heads.

At that point we hired two native Indians to guide us. Those guys were amazing— the cold didn't seem to affect them. They got us out to the lake— it took all day; we never even would have found it, even with the maps we had; but it wasn't the lake that we were trying to get to. That one was twenty miles further away and the machines kept breaking down. Our guides assured us that *fish good here,* and so we gave it a try.

We drilled holes through four feet of snow and three feet of ice, set up the portable shelters and put our small space-heaters inside them. Now we were ready to fish. When we tried to light the heaters, the kerosene wouldn't burn— it was too cold! So, without heat, we fished about thirty minutes, caught one small fish, and returned to the bank to set up camp.

We were in survival mode by then. In order to have any heat someone had to feed the fire constantly and so we took shifts— one man chopping and dragging back wood while the others sat on the ground... not talking to each other. The Indians, on the other hand, seemed unaffected by our situation. They talked and joked and seemed to be having a good time. Living up there for generations, their views on life in general were different from ours. I remember asking one of them if he had any children. He said no, he and his wife couldn't have any— but that was OK because Fred (the other indian), gave him two of his.

The next day Steve and Buddy decided to try to make it to the original lake that we had wanted to fish. Pete and I stayed at camp to keep the fire going. Once again it took them all day to get there and they came back with no fish.

At that point we decided to go home— back to the US of A where it was warmer!

The next morning all four snowmobiles were up and running and we prepared for the sixty mile ride back to our beloved plywood shack. About a half mile into the ride a machine quit and another broke down a half mile after that. Steve and Pete continued on while Buddy and I stayed back to repair the broken units. We got one running and rode it back to the lodge that night.

It was ten p.m. when we were all finally gathered back at the shack. We had lost one snowmobile and caught one small walleye for the entire trip. Everyone was exhausted and went right to sleep— ready to head home the next day. Overnight, the indians went out and retrieved the other snowmobile for us. They were enjoying themselves out there where we would have lain down and died!

After all this, any semblance of humor was gone… we were not having any *fun* anymore.

At ten a.m. the next morning we were packing up to leave. Then the suburban wouldn't start and it took five hours to get it running, but neither the front nor back heater was working. We wanted to drive the two hundred and fifty miles of *winter road* at night, when the trucks weren't running back and forth to the oil fields and softening up the road— thinking we might make better time.

We left the lodge at seven p.m., with no heat. The windows had to be left partially open to keep interior frost at a minimum— but even then it required constant scraping to be able to see outside at all. Everyone wore their snowmobile suits and got inside down sleeping bags— except, of course, the driver; he had to get out every twenty minutes and move around in order to restore circulation to his legs. I drove most of the way and could never get over ten to fifteen miles per hour— it was just too rough. I don't know what the temperature was, but Pete had on two down sleeping bags over his suit and still ended up with pretty severe frostbite.

When we finally got to the good road, still 100 miles from Winnipeg, we stopped to survey the damage. Our gear was all smashed up and the generator was missing. It just fell of somewhere back in the woods— and we never even got it started!

We had a new truck heater installed in Winnipeg and got some needed welding done on the trailer so that we could continue on.

Finally back in the U.S., we stopped in Grand Forks for a hot breakfast— our first hot meal in days. When we returned to the Suburban, both batteries were dead. We bought new ones and continued on. By then, we pretty much hated each other— we didn't want to have any more *fun*!

Late that afternoon, just ten miles north of our farm, we came over a hill and ran into a herd of deer that were just laying in the road. The impact killed two and completely wrecked the Suburban— but it would still just barely run. We limped onward, determined to just get home.

We made it, dead tired and irritable, but home. As we were unloading our gear, just to add insult to injury, the old dog that hung around the place jumped in the back of our trailer, grabbed the fish, and ran away with it!

I don't think any of us talked to each other for at least six months after that."

Dave's coke was now empty and the light was starting to fade outside. What can one say to a story like that? Only that I concurred completely… "You'r right Dave, that WAS the ice fishing trip from hell!"

The Tank

It is October in North Dakota. A north wind is howling straight out of Saskatchewan bringing one of the season's first peltings of snow. I lean into it and button the flap that holds my collar up: it doesn't help much. I am just going across the yard to check on the bird dogs in their kennels. They stay in their houses even as I approach—smart dogs. They need a little reassurance that the world is not ending and the sun will shine again on another day. I enter the pen and sit down on the elevated platform where their houses rest. Both dogs, Mary and Piper, bolt from their warm houses and jump in my lap. It is a squeeze, but they know how to handle it from long practice; Mary noses under my right arm, Piper under the left, and each puts her front paws on the nearest leg and leans in, shivering.

I usually sit awhile, like this, on days that we don't run. We just sit, and watch, and listen. They can both hear a lot better than I, and they see anything that has feathers. Sometimes rooster pheasants crow at us from just outside the fence, or geese, ducks, and cranes give voice to their own individual music as they wing their way southward— usually in curious formations— and all the while riding the great north wind. Today a flock of sharp-tailed grouse came gliding over the old barn and lit in the tall wormwood nearby. They don't usually go into such heavy cover, but I guess it's all about the wind today– thermal cover.

Near where the grouse went, and right up against the barn, is an old boat. Painted, repainted, scratched, patched and mostly hidden by wormwood weed, it has obviously not been recently used. The snow is sticking to the cold metal and who knows if the old boat will be seen again before spring?

I don't know what it would be worth as scrap metal, I hear aluminum is pretty high, but that's not what is going to happen. You see, old boats, boats that have been with you a long time and through many adventures, have souls. It is the same thing as with an old Labrador that was really good at one time; (Note: all old Labradors are thought of by their owners as really good at one time—remember Marley?) or maybe a horse that gave years of faithful service, but is now too old to work.

One can hardly keep from reminiscing in the presence of such icons...

When Daddy had our first ever, very own boat delivered to Hatchie Coon, I was ecstatic. Fifteen feet long with high sides and a pointed bow—it was a beast. Most of the boats in use back then were fourteen footers, and square fronted— this boat could haul a load and get through rough water. It had more ribs than usual, for extra strength, which I thought would make it hold up better when bashing through trees in the woods. I called it The Tank.

Many years of faithful service did this craft perform, and flawlessly kept a perfect safety record. We kids could stand up in it, jump up and down, or all stand on one gunwale and it would keep upright. Running full speed through thick willows with the three-inch trunks slamming right and left off the bow like sledgehammer blows never fazed it. Jumping stumps and beaver dams, sometimes at full speed, were everyday occurrences. All in all it was, in my mind, a tank.

Occasionally, through the years, the old boat went on other adventures: a ride in the back of the truck to Pawleys Island, South Carolina, for flounder, clams and bluefish—I can still taste those clams, fresh dug and steamed in seaweed with lemon and butter, if I close my eyes and try, or hear the bluefish beating out their death-throws on the dented and scarred bottom of the boat. Another year a trip was made to Orange Beach, Alabama, because the big blues were hanging out in the pass that year—there is a large dent in the bow, on the left side, caused by a wave slamming us into the rocks of the jetty while we were trying to extricate a fouled anchor in rough seas. We lost that one. Other excursions were made in home waters: fishing, frogging, exploration, duck and dove hunting on numerous rivers and lakes, wherever we wanted to go, The Tank was ready.

Eventually the old and battered craft retired to my dad's house and received a Tennessee boat registration sticker over all the old Arkansas numbers. Years went by with no activity until one day Daddy called up and said that he and Mom were downsizing, and did I want the old boat?

A Mississippi sticker was placed over the others and new numbers were painted on the sides. Duck hunting trips were made on the Mississippi River with a long-tailed Go-Devil on the back; plowing through dense vegetation on the big river's willow bars, The Tank seemed happy being useful again.

Eventually, the boy grew older and moved to North Dakota. Somehow, with all the other stuff on the trailer, The Tank made the trip. A fourth state now had claim to the registration.

It had actually been quite a few years since I had used the old boat. During this period I had somehow managed to gain in bulk, and, apparently, lose in balance. When I put it in the water I was astonished at how small it was, and how tippy! Water poured in through most of the rivets and the transom was so low that wave-splash could easily come over the top. I patched her up as best I could, put a six-horse on the back—at one time I had run a thirty-five horse Johnson on this boat—and used it that way for a duck and goose hunting season on nearby Horsehead Lake. The leaks continued, a crack or two appeared, and The Tank was retired to its present resting place.

.... The snow is still falling, but the wind has abated somewhat. Lost in the chronology I have sat here too long. My knees creak when I stand up and I have to be careful when ducking out of the gate—three back surgeries have left me none too supple; I turn and give one last look toward the barn.

The old boat lies beside the barn like an old dog—too decrepit to hunt, but full of memories, good ones too... like a lot of us, and it will stay there for as long as I am here.

I hope that you have enjoyed this book. It is a labor of love for me to write one but to get it into print is a lot of work. It would be a favor to me if you would Tweet, Facebook, or just tell someone about it— try to get the word out!

This title and another by the author— "Take Me Back"— can be purchased on Amazon, in book stores, from the printer— https://www.createspace.com/4774698 for "The Family Jewels", or https://www.createspace.com/3713209 for "Take Me Back", or from me. Both titles are soon to be available on Kindle!

Charles B. Neely

"Buck Neely"

buckneely@gmail.com

address: 1226 Lula-Moonlake rd.

Dundee, Ms. 38626